D041696B

SHETLAND
ISLANDS

FAIR
ISLE

ORKNEY
ISLANDS

GRAMPIAN
MOUNTAINS

NORTH SEA

Edinburgh

CHEVIOT
HILLS

Tyne

Tees

PENNINES

LAKE
DISTRICT

Humber

Liverpool

THE
WASH

Mersey

Manchester

Trent

Ouse

Dee

Severn

E N G L A N D

MOUNTAINS

W A L E S

London

Thames

Dover

Cardiff

ISLE
OF
WIGHT

ENGLISH CHANNEL

CHANNEL
ISLANDS

BRITAIN

BRITAIN

By the Editors of Time-Life Books

TIME-LIFE BOOKS · AMSTERDAM

HEALTHY HOME COOKING
UNDERSTANDING COMPUTERS
THE ENCHANTED WORLD
LIBRARY OF NATIONS
HOME REPAIR AND IMPROVEMENT
CLASSICS OF EXPLORATION
PLANET EARTH
PEOPLES OF THE WILD
THE EPIC OF FLIGHT
THE SEAFARERS
WORLD WAR II
THE GOOD COOK
THE TIME-LIFE ENCYCLOPAEDIA
OF GARDENING
THE GREAT CITIES
THE OLD WEST
THE WORLD'S WILD PLACES
THE EMERGENCE OF MAN
LIFE LIBRARY OF PHOTOGRAPHY
TIME-LIFE LIBRARY OF ART
GREAT AGES OF MAN
LIFE SCIENCE LIBRARY
LIFE NATURE LIBRARY
THE TIME-LIFE BOOK OF BOATING
TECHNIQUES OF PHOTOGRAPHY
LIFE AT WAR
LIFE GOES TO THE MOVIES
BEST OF LIFE
LIFE IN SPACE

TIME-LIFE BOOKS

EUROPEAN EDITOR: Kit van Tulleken
Assistant European Editor: Gillian Moore
Design Director: Ed Skyner
Chief of Research: Vanessa Kramer
Chief Sub-Editor: Ilse Gray

LIBRARY OF NATIONS

Series Editor: Tony Allan

Editorial Staff for *Britain*
Editor: Gillian Moore
Researcher: Margaret Hall
Designer: Mary Staples
Sub-Editor: Sally Rowland
Picture Department: Christine Hinze, Peggy Tout
Editorial Assistant: Molly Oates

EDITORIAL PRODUCTION

Chief: Jane Hawker
Traffic Co-ordinators: Alan Godwin, Maureen Kelly
Editorial Department: Theresa John, Debra Lelliott, Sylvia Osborne

© 1985 Time-Life Books B.V. All rights reserved.
Second European English language printing 1987.

No part of this book may be reproduced in any form or by any electronic or mechanical means, including information storage and retrieval devices or systems, without prior written permission from the publisher, except that brief passages may be quoted for review.

ISBN 7054 0845 0

TIME-LIFE is a trademark of Time Incorporated U.S.A.

CONSULTANTS: A. H. Halsey, Ph.D., is Professor of Social and Administrative Studies at the University of Oxford and a fellow of Nuffield College, Oxford. He has written numerous books and articles on class, education and social change in Britain.

Anthony Sampson is the author of *Anatomy of Britain*—a survey of British institutions—and several sequels, the most recent of which is *The Changing Anatomy of Britain*. He has also written books on the European Community, banking, international corporations and the oil industry.

Special Contributors: The chapter texts were written by: Windsor Chorlton, Anthony Hilton, Alan Lothian and Michael Ratcliffe.

Other contributors: Christopher Farman, Deborah Thompson.

Cover: Spring sunlight catches the steep roofs of a row of 17th-century cottages in the village of Bibury in Gloucestershire. Situated on the limestone ridge of the Cotswold Hills, the village is built from the local honey-coloured stone.

Pages 1 and 2: The armorial bearings of the Monarch who, as Head of State, symbolizes the British nation, are shown on page 1. On the following page appears Britain's national flag, the Union Jack, which combines the crosses of St. George of England, St. Andrew of Scotland and St. Patrick of Ireland.

Front and back endpapers: A topographical map showing the major rivers, mountain ranges and other natural features of Britain appears on the front endpaper; the back endpaper shows the counties and principal towns.

This volume is one in a series of books describing countries of the world—their natural resources, peoples, histories, economies and governments.

CONTENTS

A shepherd and his well-disciplined flock progress along a road in the Yorkshire moors towards fresh pasture. Hardy breeds of sheep thrive in such

GROWING YIELDS FROM AGRICULTURE

Like other countries in the European Economic Community, Britain has achieved a rising agricultural output in recent years despite a small drop in the number of people employed in farming. The growth has been particularly marked since Britain entered the Community in 1973 and farmers were obliged to compete directly with their European neighbours for markets. To meet the challenge, they invested heavily in new machines and techniques, and many of them enlarged their holdings. Britain now possesses one of Europe's most productive rural sectors: only the Netherlands and Belgium boast a higher agriculture output per worker.

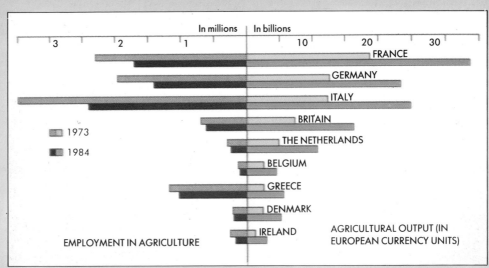

In millions | In billions

3   2   1   10   20   30

FRANCE
GERMANY
ITALY
BRITAIN
THE NETHERLANDS
BELGIUM
GREECE
DENMARK
IRELAND

■ 1973
■ 1984

EMPLOYMENT IN AGRICULTURE

AGRICULTURAL OUTPUT (IN EUROPEAN CURRENCY UNITS)

upland zones as this, but the major sheep-rearing areas are the rich lowlands of south-west England and the Midlands.

A POPULOUS NATION

At around 230 people per square kilometre, the population density of Britain is the fourth highest in Europe, after the Netherlands, Belgium and West Germany. Nearly one third of the 56 million people live in south-east England, near London. Other crowded areas are those where coal deposits have long drawn heavy industry—south Wales, central and northern England, and central Scotland. By contrast, much of Wales and Scotland is quite empty—as is Northern Ireland, apart from industrial Belfast.

0–70
70–250
250–500
500–1,000
Over 1,000

Glasgow

Belfast

Manchester

Birmingham

London

PEOPLE PER SQUARE KILOMETRE

Evening sunlight highlights rows of 19th-century houses in Islington, north London. More than 60 per cent of British homes are owned by the occupiers;

some are outright proprietors, many are paying off a mortgage subsidized by tax allowances. Public housing accounts for a further 30 per cent of homes.

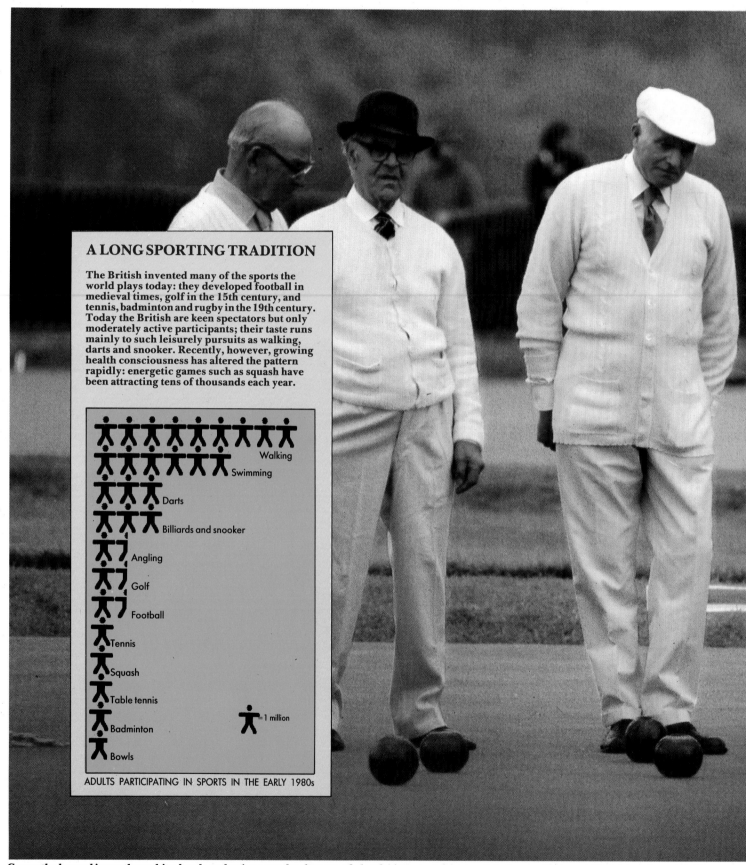

A LONG SPORTING TRADITION

The British invented many of the sports the world plays today: they developed football in medieval times, golf in the 15th century, and tennis, badminton and rugby in the 19th century. Today the British are keen spectators but only moderately active participants; their taste runs mainly to such leisurely pursuits as walking, darts and snooker. Recently, however, growing health consciousness has altered the pattern rapidly: energetic games such as squash have been attracting tens of thousands each year.

Walking

Swimming

Darts

Billiards and snooker

Angling

Golf

Football

Tennis

Squash

Table tennis

= 1 million

Badminton

Bowls

ADULTS PARTICIPATING IN SPORTS IN THE EARLY 1980s

Correctly dressed in spotless white, bowls enthusiasts ponder the state of play during a match in a park in the seaside town of Brighton. Associated in past

centuries with drinking, gambling and rowdy behaviour, bowls today is an eminently respectable sport, and especially popular among the elderly.

PROFITS FROM POP

Since the early 1960s, when the Beatles and the Rolling Stones achieved fame, Britain has produced an endless stream of creative pop musicians. A huge export industry has been built on their talents and the skills of the best recording engineers in the world.

Throughout the 1960s and early 1970s, British recordings accounted for around a quarter of world record sales. In the late 1970s, British bands met a brief reversal in their quest for international stardom: the punk and New Wave styles sweeping Britain found little favour abroad. But by the start of the 1980s, a new generation of British musicians had found world renown, appealing especially to teenage audiences. In the U.S., British names once more regularly appeared high in the charts and British groups cornered a third of the record market.

During a concert by a punk band at a London nightclub, some of the audience dance and others crowd below the stage. Deriving from rock-and-roll but

distinguished by violent rhythms and frenzied shouting, the punk sound is one of a rapid succession of waves in British pop.

In a Midlands colliery, a worker operates a shearer that traverses the coal face, slicing off gigantic slabs of the mineral and spraying out water to suppress

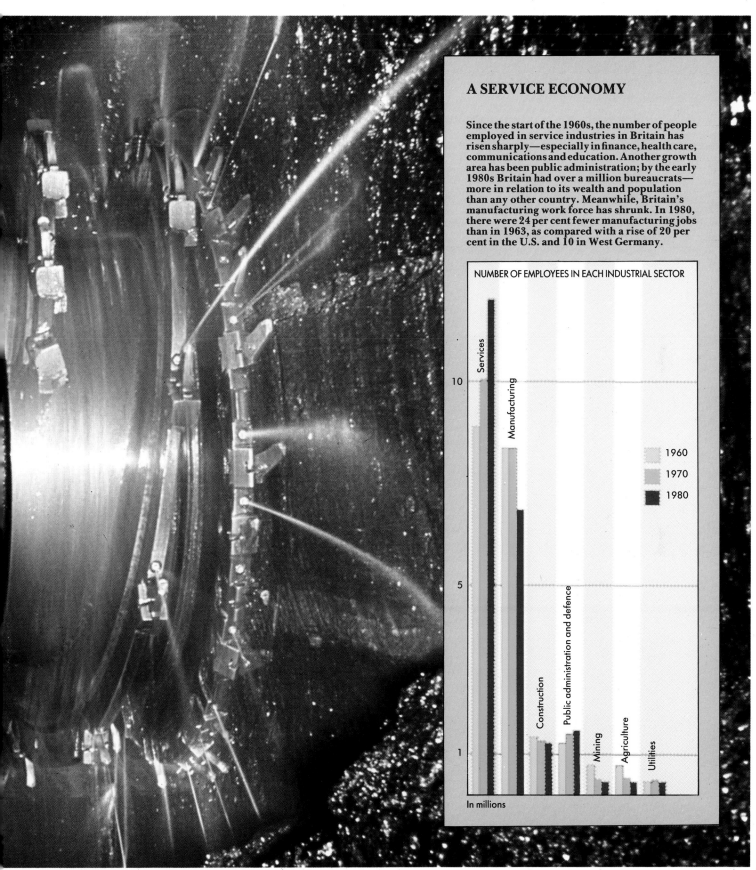

A SERVICE ECONOMY

Since the start of the 1960s, the number of people employed in service industries in Britain has risen sharply—especially in finance, health care, communications and education. Another growth area has been public administration; by the early 1980s Britain had over a million bureaucrats—more in relation to its wealth and population than any other country. Meanwhile, Britain's manufacturing work force has shrunk. In 1980, there were 24 per cent fewer manufacturing jobs than in 1963, as compared with a rise of 20 per cent in the U.S. and 10 in West Germany.

NUMBER OF EMPLOYEES IN EACH INDUSTRIAL SECTOR

Services

Manufacturing

1960
1970
1980

10

5

Construction

Public administration and defence

Mining

Agriculture

Utilities

1

In millions

dust. With such machines, Britain is at the forefront of mining technology; improved productivity has contributed to a drop in employment in mining.

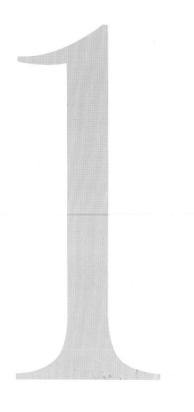

A KINGDOM OF CONTRASTS

Undulating across Northumberland, the ruins of a wall built by the Roman emperor Hadrian mark the ancient frontier between Roman Britain and the Celtic lands to the north. Hadrian's Wall is the most spectacular symbol of the tribal and political antagonisms that once cleaved Great Britain.

It is not a very big country: at 244,100 square kilometres, Britain is smaller than Italy, West Germany and 10 of the American states, and less than half the size of France. It is crowded, but not desperately so: with a population of 56 million, the population density is not as high as in Japan and Belgium, though it far exceeds that of France and the United States. Its climate is milder than its northerly latitude would suggest, thanks to the warm Gulf Stream washing its shores. The landscape, too, is gentle: ice sheets that ground across Britain some 10,000 years ago flattened its mountains, and the highest—Ben Nevis, in the misty Scottish highlands—barely tops 1,300 metres.

While Britain is a country of few extremes, the British people until a generation or two ago seemed cast on a more glorious scale. They had made themselves masters of a global empire that, at its peak in 1933, included a quarter of the world's population; their enormous possessions brought them power and influence out of all proportion to the resources of their native islands. They had industrialized 50 years before any other nation, and the lead meant that in the 1950s they were among the richest people in the world, and Europe's greatest trading nation.

Since then, however, the British have lost their pre-eminence, both political and economic. The Empire has been dismantled. Queen Elizabeth II, the great-great-granddaughter of Queen Victoria, Empress of India, is merely Head of the Commonwealth—a title with little consequence. The successive British governments which she nominally heads participate (not always with enthusiasm) in the affairs of the European Economic Community and (more wholeheartedly) in NATO. The economy has expanded—the average Briton is twice as rich as 30 years ago—but other countries have managed faster growth, and the various international comparisons of wealth, all calculated in slightly different ways, nowadays place Britain between portions 10 and 15 in their rankings.

Despite the change in their fortunes, the British have remained remarkably contented and loyal to their country. A recent poll comparing attitudes in the U.S., Japan and Europe showed that 55 per cent of Britons were "very proud" of their nation; only the Americans and the Irish surpassed them in patriotism. Another poll examined life-satisfaction in all the countries. Thirty-six per cent of Britons pronounced themselves "very satisfied" with life, as compared with 16 per cent of French respondents and 20 per cent of Germans. And in international surveys of suicide levels and crimes of violence, the British score comfortably low.

While the British still stand out in such comparisons, in most other respects they can be described without superlatives. Like their country, today's Britons avoid extremes. And yet Bri-

Trees, flowers and ample lawns preserve an illusion of rural life for the residents of Hillingdon, a commuter suburb about 30 kilometres from central London. Similar houses with spacious gardens encircle towns and cities all over Britain.

tain and the British are far from uniform. Within the limited compass of a medium-sized, urbanized industrial nation, there is extraordinary variety.

The landscapes, for example, are far more diverse than might be expected of a small island kingdom. Other countries have grander mountains, wider rivers, more spectacular coasts, but few have such a concentrated spectrum of features; hills and moorland, river and coastline, plain and woodland are crammed into such a small space that a day's journey can cover them all.

The much maligned weather is as unpredictable as the topography. Climatologists call it "cool temperate", meaning that it does not show extremes of cold or heat, rainfall or drought. Indeed Britain has one of the most equable climates in the world. London's mean temperature in July is only 13°C warmer than the January mean; the capital's rainfall, at 612 mm per year, is well under New York's, slightly more than San Francisco's, about the same as Rome's and evenly spread throughout the year. But such statistics hardly do justice to a phenomenon that provides the most unfailing topic of conversation in Britain. Climatically speaking, Britain has more accurately been called a battleground, invaded and conquered by one air mass after another and thus subject to frequent and possible stormy changes of weather in the course of a single day.

The people, equally, are more diverse than in most places of similar size, for Britain is a multinational society within a unitary political state. The island of Great Britain comprises three countries—England, Wales and Scotland. These three, together with the province of Northern Ireland, form the United Kingdom of Great Britain and

Northern Ireland. Surrounding Great Britain are many small islands, among them the Isle of Wight off southern England and Anglesey near the Welsh coast, which form part of the United Kingdom. To add to the constitutional complexity of the nation, the Isle of Man in the Irish Sea and the Channel Islands near the French coast fall outside its direct jurisdiction; they are dependencies of the British Crown with their own legislative and tax systems.

The term "United Kingdom" is rarely used in everyday language, even by those who live within its boundaries. When abroad, the peoples of these islands will probably identify their homeland as "Britain" if responding to an official enquiry; if the questioning is more personal they will say Wales, Scotland, England or Northern Ire-

land. And if a Welshman or a Scotsman is mistaken for an Englishman, he is likely to be offended. Due to their geography, culture, traditions and languages, Scotland and Wales are distinct from England; Northern Ireland, by its troubled history as part of colonial Ireland, is even more so.

Outsiders grappling with these demarcations are not helped by an old habit among the English of talking as if Britain and England were one and the same thing. Shakespeare, for example, wrote of "this sceptred isle ... this England"—he can be partly forgiven since he was writing before the four countries had been joined in a single political unit, and at least he had the tact to use the word "Briton" in *Macbeth*, written soon after the Union of the English and Scottish Crowns in 1603.

The ethnic divisions of the peoples of Britain have their roots deep in the nation's history, when the island was settled by successive waves of invaders. Four peoples—the Celts, Saxons, Vikings and Normans—made major contributions to the British stock. The first to arrive, almost 3,000 years ago, were the Celts, who in the course of the first millennium B.C. spread throughout Europe from a homeland north of the Alps. In Britain, they found and partly displaced an older, more mysterious race—the heirs of ancient cultures that some 1,000 years before had raised a great circle of standing stones at Stonehenge in Wiltshire, for use perhaps as a temple, perhaps even as an observatory, and equally enigmatic megaliths and chambered tombs at the other end of Britain, in Orkney and Caithness. The earlier inhabitants had, by the time the Celts arrived in Britain, learnt the use of bronze; the Celts introduced

Built in the 1890s and one of London's most famous landmarks, Tower Bridge is the farthest downstream of the capital's 18 road bridges. The central span consists of two drawbridges that can be raised to allow ocean-going vessels through to the docks nearby.

them to iron swords and shields.

At the end of the second century B.C., a fresh wave of Celtic invaders, the Belgic tribes, established a martial aristocracy in southern England led by warriors who charged into battle in chariots, often naked and painted with a blue dye called woad. These tribes had a priestly class, the Druids, who worshipped the moon from shrines in groves of oak, and appeased malevolent forces with human sacrifices.

We know such details of Celtic life chiefly from the Romans, who were the next foreigners to reach British shores and the first to document what they found. In 43 A.D. the legions of Claudius annexed Britain to the Roman Empire: for the next 400 years, a Roman army of 60,000 men maintained imperial control over a population of some five million. Their sway was limited to the lowlands; they left the mountainous north and west of Britain to the wild tribesmen. Even in the area where they were masters, the Romans hardly came into contact with the Celtic population, since they preferred to rule through native chiefs who assumed Roman ways. When they were forced to leave Britain to defend their own country from barbarian attacks, they left behind little tangible evidence of their long occupation except a fine network of roads and military camps.

In the wake of the Romans came a new wave of invaders—this time Jutes from present-day Denmark, Angles from where Hamburg is today, Saxons from north Germany and Frisians from the Netherlands. By the early seventh century, the newcomers—referred to generically by historians as Anglo-Saxons or Saxons—had conquered almost all of England and, unlike the Romans, they stayed. They did not penetrate the wilder regions to the north and west, so Scotland, Ireland, Wales and the western tip of England remained the province of the Celts.

Although the Saxons were obviously warriors of prowess, it was as farmers that they left a lasting mark on the landscape. They cleared much of the forest that still covered the country; introduced a heavy plough which remained virtually unchanged until the

1

Celt alike in their zeal for booty. The natives lived in terror of the dragon-prowed longships that loomed out of the fog, discharging fearsome swordsmen who sacked farms and churches, murdered monks and raped women. Fortunately, before the Vikings destroyed the British civilizations, they were seduced by the settled life of their victims. The pagan seafaring warriors

that had succeeded Canute, and he laid claim to the throne of England. In 1066, he crossed the English Channel with 8,000 men and conquered the Saxons at the Battle of Hastings. William crowned himself king of England in London. He imposed a feudal structure on English society and inevitably the uppermost tiers were occupied by Normans. Scotland, Wales and Ireland remained Celtic strongholds.

The racial pattern completed by 1066 is still visible today. The Scots, the Welsh and the Irish revel in the romance of their Celtic ancestry. English culture developed out of a fusion of Saxon, Viking and Norman traditions, though the English like to stress their Saxon heritage and see themselves as descendants of the pragmatic Saxon farmers. The caricature Englishman has long been the corpulent country squire John Bull, a conservative, home-loving, down-to-earth fellow.

While ancient racial differences thus account for much of the diversity with-

Agricultural Revolution in the 18th century; and established settlements that were so carefully sited they have survived until the present day.

England was becoming a peaceful, prosperous place and the civilizing process was hastened by the spread of Christianity. In 597 St. Augustine was sent on a missionary journey to England by Pope Gregory I. Augustine established the ecclesiastical capital at Canterbury, where it has remained. In the north, a slightly different form of Christianity was brought by Irish and Scots missionaries, whose Celtic artistic influence enriched the illuminated scriptures by the monks of Northumbria and the Scottish island of Iona.

In the eighth and ninth centuries, raiders from across the North Sea came near to obliterating this vigorous culture. Viking warriors—at first from Norway, then Denmark—mounted attacks on almost every stretch of Britain's coastline, harrowing Saxon and

found in eastern England a resting place, married with the local Saxon population, took up farming and allowed themselves to be converted to Christianity. The Danish king Canute became king of all England in 1016; his wise rule sealed the reconciliation of the Saxon and Viking populations.

The last invaders of Britain were the Normans—again a people of Viking stock, who had settled in northern France in the 10th century and adopted the French language and the Christian religion. William, Duke of Normandy, was related to the English royal line in the British population, they are far from providing the complete story. The history of the last 900 years has also helped to mould regional character. And the most notable fact of history is that during those 900 years, power came to be centred in England. The Welsh, the Scots and the Irish all found themselves subjected, in varying degrees, to England's political will.

Wales was the first of the three formally to lose its sovereignty. The early Norman kings of England demanded an oath of fealty from Wales's princes, but left them to rule their mountain strongholds until, in 1275, Prince Llywelyn ap Gruffyd and his brother David revolted. Edward I of England quelled their revolt and in 1284 made Wales subject to the English crown. From the 16th century, Wales was represented in the Parliament in London, and the Welsh shared as equal partners in the nation's government.

Scotland resisted domination for much longer, fighting repeated battles

The diversity of racial strains in Britain is reflected in these six portraits. Few features are sure guides to ancestry, but black skin *(above)* probably means West Indian descent while red hair *(top, right)* often signifies Scots or Irish blood.

against English armies. When the country was eventually united with England, it was not by force but by a political expedient. In 1603, when Elizabeth I, the Virgin Queen, died heirless, James VI of Scotland became ruler of England by an accident of blood lineage: he was the only surviving descendant of the English king Henry VII, who had founded the Tu-

dor dynasty. As England's James I, he moved his court to England and lived there for most of the rest of his life.

Although his successors, too, stayed in England, Scotland retained its own governing assembly in Edinburgh for a century after the Union of Crowns. By the end of the 17th century, the most influential people in Scotland believed that their country could only prosper if its political links with England were strengthened, and in 1707 the Treaty of the Union of Parliaments was ratified. There was now a Parliament of Great Britain at Westminster in London,

which consisted of representatives from England, Wales and Scotland.

Scotland kept some of its own institutions, which remain among its distinguishing features to this day. The first was its legal system. While the basis of English law is the "common law" founded on precedence, the system in Scotland, as in much of continental Europe, is founded on Roman law. So whenever a piece of legislation is intended to apply to Scotland as well as England and Wales, a separate appendix or even a separate measure has to be passed. One result is that the law in Scotland is not always identified with that in England and Wales.

Another concession to Scotland was in the matter of religion. In England, the established church since the English Reformation of 1534 had been the Church of England which, though Protestant, retained the ecclesiastical hierarchy of bishops and archbishops inherited from the Roman church. But

1

in Scotland at the time of the Union of Parliaments, the dominant faith was and continued to be Presbyterianism, a form of Calvinism, in which ministers are elected by the congregation. Scotland also kept its own arrangements for local government and education.

Since the 12th century, when Henry II of England invaded Ireland, that country's history has been a bitter tale of resistance to English, then British rule. England never really treated Ireland as an integral part of the United Kingdom, rather as a colony to be exploited, and Ireland was not formally united with England, Scotland and Wales until 1800. This colonial experience helped to keep alive a powerful nationalist sentiment, which erupted in the Easter Rising of 1916 when a small group of republicans tried to set up a provisional government but capitulated after a few days. The Anglo-Irish Treaty of 1921 granted Home Rule to the Catholic south (it became a republic in 1949), leaving Ulster, or Northern Ireland—where Protestants predominated—within the United Kingdom.

Thus through conquest or consent, Wales, Scotland and, for a time, Ireland became part of one kingdom. In theory, all the constituent countries were to be equal partners in the running of the realm. In practice, because England has been not only the seat of government but also the richest and most populous country, it has dominated the others, which frequently complain of being exploited, misunderstood or simply forgotten.

Within England, a similar pattern appears in miniature. London, the capital, is the city of government and the site of many industries' head offices; moreover, it is situated in the southeast, England's wealthiest region. In

Beyond a field of stubble in the Kent countryside, trellises support vine-like hop plants—cultivated for the bitter flavour they add to beer. In the background, the crooked ventilation spires of the oast house where the hops are dried rise above a meadow.

Stepped 18th-century houses in Shaftesbury sit high above the lush farmlands of Dorset. Under its old name, Shaston, the town features in the works of the 19th-century novelist Thomas Hardy.

the rest of the country London inspires envy and mistrust in equal measure. And with some justice: though four countries are represented in London, London is typical of nothing but itself.

London is the product of accretion—the slow accumulation of wealth, power, land and people. Founded by the Romans at the highest point on the River Thames to which seagoing ships could sail, it quickly became Britain's leading port. For the first 1,000 years of its existence, it occupied under 3 square kilometres, bounded by the Thames and the stout walls the Romans had built. Today, London's ancient core, known as the City, houses a high proportion of the nation's great financial institutions. Sleek glass skyscrapers jostle with ponderous Victorian piles—but the tortuous streetplan is inherited from the Middle Ages, and Roman ruins lie at the foot of the soaring office blocks.

In late medieval times, the City burst its walls and spread westwards to impinge on the village of Westminster—for long the residence of kings and the seat of government, today dominated by the Victorian Gothic

spires of the Houses of Parliament. Burgeoning growth continued: at the beginning of the 17th century, London was a city of 100,000 people and had expanded south of the Thames. Shakespeare lived on the south bank and here too stood the Globe Theatre, which held the first performances of many of his works. Thereafter London spread in every direction, absorbing village after outlying village—Marylebone in the 18th century, Kensington, Chelsea and Hampstead in the 19th, leafy Richmond and Hampton in the 20th. Some of the intervening spaces were developed on a grand scale with a unifying design; the harmonious squares and terraces of Bloomsbury, Mayfair and Belgravia resulted from such ventures. But there has never been an overall plan for London as there was for New York or Paris; the separate settlements retain their own character, giving London the air of a collection of villages.

The illusion of village life is affirmed by London's low housing density. Britons have never greatly taken to living in flats and even Londoners aspire to a house—and a plot of land—of their own. As a result, large parts of London

are covered by dwellings no more than three or four floors high, with a garden behind and sometimes in front as well. To supplement their private resources of greenery, Londoners have access to 160 square kilometres of parks, most of them former royal hunting grounds. No other major capital is so endowed with open spaces. There is a price to pay for the inner-city illusions of countryside thus created, however, and that is the distance at which many of the capital's inhabitants live from the real countryside. The 1981 population of London, at 6.7 million, was less than that of New York or Tokyo, but because Londoners insist on space, the Greater London area spreads over 1,500 square kilometres—twice the area of New York and almost three times that of Tokyo.

At the end of the Second World War, with large parts of central London flattened by bombs, a radical plan to halt the capital's amoeba-like growth was put into action. To reduce the inner-city population, superior housing was offered in eight new towns, separated from the suburban fringe by a green belt of undisturbed countryside on to which the London conurbation was not allowed to expand. Even now, the original new towns, plus others, continue to grow, while many older towns in the south-east are also spreading rapidly to absorb London's overspill.

The capital itself—in common with most of Britain's older cities—has been shrinking. Between 1971 and 1981, London's population fell by 10.1 per cent, to less than the figure for 1901. In parts of the inner city, the population fell by as much as a quarter, leaving a disproportionately large number of immigrants, the poor and the elderly. The decline was due partly to a falling birth rate, partly to a sharp decrease in the

number of industrial jobs in London. And many Londoners left simply because the capital had got too big, too noisy and too expensive.

Yet London is a long way from dying. Indeed, it accommodates areas of excellence and energy found in few other metropolises. With more than 100 theatres, several hundred publishing houses and a dozen major concert halls, it is unquestionably one of Europe's foremost centres of high and popular culture. And though no longer the headquarters of a world empire, it maintains a global outlook. Heathrow, London's main airport, handles more international traffic than any other; the British Broadcasting Corporation transmits radio programmes worldwide in over 30 languages; and the City exploits the business opportunities offered by Britain's longitudinal position midway between the other giants of finance, the U.S. and Japan: a deal can be broached in a morning telephone call to Japan, discussed in the afternoon call to New York and clinched by the end of London's working day.

Many of those who take part in London's vigorous daytime activities are not there to enjoy its nightlife: 400,000 commuters pour in and out of London by train every day and thousands more endure the journey by car. The counties surrounding London are full of towns that are hardly more than dormitories for the capital.

George Orwell, writing in 1938, called the counties south of London "the sleekest landscape in the world"—a place where he found it difficult "to believe that anything is really happening anywhere. Earthquakes in Japan, famines in China, revolution in Mexico? Don't worry, the milk will be on the doorstep tomorrow morning."

For Orwell, a socialist just returned from horrors of the Spanish Civil War, it was the English idyll of his childhood—"the railway cuttings smothered in wild flowers, the deep meadows where the great shining horses browse and meditate, the slow-moving streams bordered by willows, the green bosoms of the elms, the larkspurs in the cottage gardens... all sleeping the deep, deep sleep of England."

Today, that sleep is broken by the hum of road traffic and the roar of aeroplanes. Many of the wild flowers have gone, poisoned by agricultural dressings; the great shining horses—there were still 300,000 working the land as late as 1950—have been replaced by shinier machines; willow-fringed streams can still be found, but most of the elms have been felled—toppled by an insidious parasite that ravaged Britain in the 1960s and 1970s; the cottages with their gardens are likely to be the weekend retreats of London advertising executives. Yet much of the old England remains: neat orchards and hop fields in Kent; drowsy thatched villages in Sussex; sheep grazing on the Downs above Brighton.

The counties bordering on London are not unique in preserving pockets of rural tranquillity amid the 20th-century bustle. Throughout Britain, the new and the old, the developed and the unspoilt, lie juxtaposed. Except in the north of Scotland, there are no extensive stretches of empty wilderness; even the grimiest industrial town in Wales or the north of England is within a few minutes' drive of green fields and hills.

To the west of London, the contrasts are particularly noticeable. Reading, Basingstoke, Newbury and Aylesbury used to be little more than sleepy, pretty market towns serving local farming communities. Today they still perform that function, but they also house scores of companies involved in computer manufacture and other new technology industries—so many, indeed, that the 300-kilometre east-west corridor between London and Bristol has been christened "silicon alley". The area owes its boom to its proximity to

24

Small pleasure boats lie moored by the more functional fishing smacks in the harbour at Polperro, a tiny village on the Cornish coast. Polperro's streets are so steep and narrow that cars have been banned from its centre.

London and to the ports and airports giving access to EEC markets, coupled with its freedom from the burden of an out-of-date industrial infrastructure. Another magnet is the lovely scenery nearby—the chalk downlands and the broad, fertile valleys of Hampshire, Wiltshire and Dorset which Thomas Hardy celebrated in his novels.

An earthwork called Bokerley Dyke on the county boundary between Dorset and Hampshire marks an ancient frontier between the territories of the native British and the invading Saxons. West of the dyke, the Celtic influence on the landscape is striking, with numerous hill forts, burial mounds and pagan figures carved into the hillsides. Cornwall, on the end of Great Britain's south-west peninsula, was England's last Celtic stronghold, where the population spoke a language similar to Welsh until the end of the 18th century. There have been demands for a revival of the Cornish culture, but they stand little chance in the face of the influx of outsiders attracted by the mild climate, sea-cut cliffs and picturesque fishing villages. Many of these incomers are retired people, making the Cornish population the most elderly in Britain. For the young, there are few job opportunities outside tourism and agriculture, and many move away.

Ironically, Cornwall may have been the first industrial site in England. In the past, the region had unusually rich deposits of tin, which the ancients alloyed with copper to make bronze for weapons and drinking vessels. Phoenicians probably bought the tin 3,000 years ago. The mines were worked until this century, but the seams have now run out and the engine houses stand empty and rusting, lending a melancholy atmosphere to the area.

A very different landscape northeast of London is East Anglia, a mainly low-lying region that contains the most fertile soil in Britain. It was here, in Norfolk and Suffolk, that an agricultural revolution was born, when 18th-century experimenters in crop rotation eliminated the fallow year that had seemed obligatory. The breakthrough came when they realized the value of fodder crops: their four-course rotation of wheat, turnips, barley and hay became the pattern throughout Europe during the 19th century.

Towards the west of Norfolk and in adjacent Cambridgeshire are found the Fenlands—treeless prairies, broken by drains and sluices, punctuated by church steeples on the few patches of high ground. Some parts of the Fens have been reclaimed from the sea, and much of the area was a marshland wilderness until the 17th century.

Though agricultural improvements made East Anglia rich during the Napoleonic wars of the early 19th century, the region went into a decline as Britain's Empire grew and the nation became accustomed to importing much of its food. World War II brought a renewed demand for home-produced food, and East Anglia was prosperous once more. In the 1970s, it was one of the few regions to show a growth in population—mainly overspill from London. Its position close to the great European ports also made it a natural choice for the development of container traffic after Britain joined the EEC.

The Midlands, stretching west from East Anglia to the Welsh border, epitomize the poet William Blake's two famous phrases about England: here the "green and pleasant land" stands cheek-by-jowl with "dark, Satanic mills". Although the region is fringed by beautiful countryside—the gentle Cotswolds hills with their villages of honey-coloured limestone, the more rugged Derbyshire Peak District and the hedgerows and coverts of Leicestershire—it is England's most intensely industrialized area, the centre of Britain's automobile and engineering industries. Its main cities—particularly Birmingham—have had their hearts torn out to make them fitting places for cars to occupy. North of Birmingham is the Black Country, named by a 19th-century American visitor who was appalled by the sight of the waste spewed out by its forges and furnaces.

To the west of Birmingham lies a sleepy village that was the first home of the Industrial Revolution. It was at Coalbrookdale, in Shropshire, that a young entrepreneur called Abraham Darby successfully used coke for the first time in iron smelting and thus laid the foundations of the modern iron industry. Between 1773 and 1779, his grandson used the techniques to construct the first iron bridge, which still spans the River Severn. These were small ventures, however, limited by local resources, and as the Industrial Revolution gained momentum, the sites of the new industries moved to the great coalfields in Staffordshire, Yorkshire, north-east England and South Wales.

On the map, Wales looks not much bigger than East Anglia, but it is a country, not a region, as is apparent to anyone who crosses the Severn Bridge, the main road route in from southern England. For a start, the road signs are in Welsh as well as English, testifying to the fact that the national language of Wales is officially recognized. It was not always so. Under Henry VIII, efforts were made to stamp out Welsh by

**Summer storm clouds and sunlight
compete over a fertile green valley
surrounded by scree-clad hills in
central Wales. In the farms and
hamlets of such valleys Welsh is still
spoken by a majority of the inhabitants.**

compelling all officeholders to speak English and by making the native tongue illegal in courts of law; and until recently it was little used in schools. That it survived is due partly to the establishment, in the early 18th century, of the non-conformist Methodist church, whose chapels are found today in every Welsh community. Welsh became the language of the pulpit, the language of the fervent hymn-singing for which the country is still famous.

The Industrial Revolution brought a large influx of English workers to the South Wales coalfields and, partly as a result, the number of Welsh-speakers declined drastically in that area. For the coalminers crammed into terraced villages in the steep valleys, class identity was a more powerful force than national sentiment, and there sprang up a political radicalism that produced the first moves towards trade unions.

South Wales is nowadays an area of industrial decline. In 1950, its valleys contained more than 150 collieries, providing one in four of all industrial jobs in Wales. By the early 1980s, the number of collieries had fallen to less than 40, and jobs were down by more than 75 per cent. A similar decline has occurred in the Welsh steel industry, which saw the loss of more than 20,000 jobs in a period of just four years. At the same time, new jobs were created in light manufacturing and the electronics industry—but not enough to halt an exodus from the valleys. Many of the old mining villages in the famous valleys of Rhondda and Merthyr have the bleak, despairing air of ghost towns.

Across the watershed of the South Wales valleys, the land gets increasingly hilly towards the north, passing from rolling sheep-walks and steep oak woods to the jagged peaks and wild scree slopes of Snowdonia. Neither Roman nor Saxon succeeded in penetrating this mountain fastness, and it is here that most of the 500,000 Welsh-speakers live. Here too, the Welsh tradition of music and verse—celebrated since 1176 at the annual gathering of poets and minstrels known as the eisteddfod—is most lovingly preserved. The Welsh pride themselves on their powers of oratory, which hark back to the chanting of their bards, and this gift for words, combined with the political radicalism born in the mining villages, explains perhaps why so many leading politicians have been Welsh.

If an imaginary line drawn along the North Wales coast were to be continued eastwards across England, it could serve as a boundary between the Midlands and the North. Nottingham and Stoke-on-Trent, not far below the line, belong unarguably to the central region; yet Sheffield, Manchester and Liverpool, only 50 kilometres away, are indisputably northern cities.

The fictional line separating these cities marks a real cultural division, for northernness is a state of mind as well as a matter of geography. Between the north and the rest of the country, there has long been a sense of rivalry, part jocular and part bitter. While the north dismisses the other regions of England, including the Midlands, as hypocritical, devious and "soft", the southerners vilify the north as crass, boorish and acquisitive. In part, these folk attitudes date back to the Industrial Revolution, and reflect the antagonism between urban and rural values—the urban being represented by the north, with its new towns blackened by factory smoke; and the rural by the south, with its rigid social hierarchy based on the possession of a long bloodline rather than on wealth. In the stereotyped view, a southerner speaks in a drawling, affected voice, while a northerner almost invariably talks in the flat accents of Lancashire or Yorkshire.

These counties lie on different sides of the Pennines, and owe their industrial development to this chain of hills. While the high rainfall on the western slopes provided abundant supplies of soft water for Lancashire's cotton industry, the drier uplands in the Pennines' rain shadow provided the sheep pastures that made Yorkshire the world's greatest woollen centre. Nowadays, both counties have had to diversify their industrial activities. Lancashire is a centre for electrical and heavy engineering, petrochemicals, pharmaceuticals and automobile production. Yorkshire owes much of its prosperity to agriculture, fishing and tourism.

Lack of industrial diversification is the besetting problem of the conurbations on the Tyne and Tees Rivers in north-east England, whose coalfields and shipyards fuelled the Industrial Revolution and supplied Britain with a large part of its iron-clad navy. Although the area set a bench-mark for dilapidation during the depression of the 1930s, little was done subsequently to diminish the dependence on traditional industries, and in the recession of the 1970s the same spectre of mass unemployment hung over the region.

From the Tyne valley, an old Roman road rises in a series of exhilarating switchbacks that climb straight as an arrow to the Northumbrian moors. For more than 1,500 years, this was no-man's land, fought over by Romans, Vikings, English and Scots. Now the sheep have it virtually to themselves, and the only hints of its bloody past are

the signs pointing to ancient battle-fields, and the fact that the few villages have large greens where cattle could be herded when the Scots came raiding.

Travelling across the border between England and Scotland—marked by no frontier guards or customs posts but by a simple road-sign welcoming the wayfarer to a new country—the visitor soon becomes aware of a subtle change, a paring away of inessentials. The stone houses are quite plain, the shops almost unadorned. Yet beyond noting this simplicity, amounting sometimes to austerity, the traveller would be wise to avoid easy generalizations. For although Scotland is no bigger than the American state of Maine, its cultural

and physical diversity are incomparably greater. There are really two Scotlands—the relatively dry and fertile Lowlands of the south and east, where most of the population and industry are concentrated, and the much wetter and more barren Highlands of the north and west, which make up nearly half of Scotland's land area yet contain only about 5 per cent of the population. This division has no formal significance today, but for most of Scotland's history the Highlands and the Lowlands were deeply divided by race and language.

In the centuries after the Norman invasion, the Lowlanders increasingly intermingled with the English, adopted Norman-English ways and, like their fellows across the border, became a

predominantly feudal society. Even the Scots hero Robert the Bruce, vanquisher of the English at the critical Battle of Bannockburn in 1314, was of Norman descent. The Highlanders, however, preserved a Celtic tribal tradition, based on the clan, whose principal feature was an absolute loyalty to a hereditary chief. They spoke Gaelic, brought from Ireland in the sixth century, lived by subsistence farming eked out by rustling raids on their Highland and Lowland neighbours, and wore their own distinctive dress, consisting of a plaid wool robe that hung to the knees like a skirt—the model for today's kilt. The hostility between Highlander and Lowlander was so fierce that not even the threat posed by their

1

mutual enemies, the English, could overcome it. During most of the wars with England, the Scottish kings also had to combat internal intrigues and rebellions mounted by Highlanders.

The Protestant Reformation introduced a new source of conflict between Highlanders and Lowlanders. In the 16th century, Calvinism spread among the Lowland Scots, but the Highlanders remained loyal to the Catholic faith or turned to the Episcopal Church, the Scots equivalent of the Church of England. The Treaty of Union with England, by guaranteeing Presbyterianism as the established religion of Scotland, intensified sectarian feeling. In 1715 and 1745, Highland sentiment erupted in rebellion led by Catholic descendants of James II, pretenders to the Scottish and English thrones. The 1745 rebellion led by Bonnie Prince Charlie was smashed in 1746 by a government army at the Battle of Culloden. Some of the rebels were executed; others, including the Prince, went into exile. After the rebellion, the Highland Scots were forbidden to wear the kilt or carry arms. All hopes of a restoration of the clan way of life were abandoned.

But less than a century later, the Highland ways came in for a nostalgic revival. The instigator of the cult was novelist Sir Walter Scott, who from 1814 wrung the world's hearts with a series of romances evoking Highland life. In 1822 he masterminded a visit to Scotland by George IV. Scott brought the royal palace of Holyrood in Edinburgh back to life and decked it out in Highland trappings, including kilts, bagpipes, banners and weapons. Even the king wore tartan. Thirty years later, the monarchy sealed its approval of Scotland with the purchase of Balmoral Castle in Aberdeenshire's Dee-

side, where the royal family still spend lengthy holidays. Following the royal fashion, England's rich industrialists bought Highland estates to follow the new sports of deer stalking, grouse shooting and salmon fishing. And every year Braemar, a village near Balmoral, attracts thousands of exiled Scots to its display of Highland music and games.

Scotland's largest city is Glasgow—an unlovely child of the Industrial Revolution which had some of the worst slums in Europe until the 1970s. The shipbuilding that fuelled Glasgow's expansion is in decline, but in the early 1980s the city received an unexpected by-product of its industrial activities: a museum of fine arts, the most important to open in Britain since World War II, built to house the collection of shipping tycoon William Burrell. The stylish building with its eclectic assemblage of beautiful objects has given the city a badly needed boost to morale.

Scotland's capital Edinburgh is only 70 kilometres from Glasgow but it seems a world apart. Its coolly classical 18th-century terraces and squares contrast stunningly with a wild gothic setting of volcanic troughs and peaks crowned with castles and spires. After the Union of Parliaments, Edinburgh lost most of the functions of a capital city and became tainted by a musty provincialism. Many of its famous sons, including the economist Adam Smith, the philosopher David Hume, the historian Thomas Carlyle and the writer Robert Louis Stevenson, chose to pursue their careers away from the city. Today, Edinburgh has regained the air of a cultural capital, whose annual international festival of the arts is the largest and best-attended in the world.

North of Edinburgh, the busiest and most prosperous city is Aberdeen, on

the east coast. A fishing port with an ancient university, the dour granite city leapt to prominence after oil was discovered in the North Sea in 1969. Aberdeen became the centre from which the oil companies directed their exploration and drilling programmes. Foreign oil experts moved into the city and the surrounding lush farmlands, and today off-duty workers from the offshore rigs roam the streets in search of entertainment. They find little except drink, for Aberdeen is curiously unchanged: it remains stolid, virtuous and chilly. The American writer Paul Theroux, visiting Aberdeen some time after the oil had begun to flow, complained that "it had all the extortionate high prices of a boom town but none of the compensating vulgarity".

Inland from the broad strip of flat land that runs up Scotland's east coast, the Scottish Highlands stretch from just north of Glasgow to the wilds of Sutherland, where weird masses of rock rise abruptly from a wilderness of moor and bog. The glens of the Highlands are achingly beautiful and hauntingly desolate, peopled by the ghosts of the clans. After Culloden, the clans' tribal way of life died a slow and lingering death. With English rule, fighting became a way of the past, and the clan chieftains, attracted by the glitter of London or Paris, demanded rent from the clansman crofter instead of the warrior service he had traditionally rendered. Since their tenants had no money, the chieftains sold or leased their lands to English landowners, who had developed new strains of sheep that could find pasture on the Scottish hills. As the sheep moved in, the crofters were moved out. Between about 1780 and 1860, while the artificial Highland cult gained momentum, the Highland

Steam from factory chimneys combines with rain to soften the stark, geometric lines of terraced houses in Colne and Nelson. The conurbation of two towns sprang up at the beginning of the 19th century to house workers in Lancashire's cotton industry.

Clearances dispossessed many thousands of real Highlanders. Some disappeared into the sprawling slums of Glasgow; many thousands emigrated to North America or Australia.

What remains of the Highland way of life can be found in Gaelic-speaking pockets on the west coast and its fringe of islands, the Hebrides. But fewer than 100,000 can speak Gaelic and it is only taught in a few schools. The Gaelic author and poet John MacDonald predicts that if the numbers dwindle at the present rate, nobody will be speaking Gaelic in 50 years.

Northern Ireland approaches the Scottish Highlands in beauty and exceeds them in its quota of human tragedy. Most of the countryside is green and gentle, with isolated farms and small, trim towns. But towards the coast the land rises steeply, culminating to the west in the breathtaking Mourne Mountains, which rise barely 3 kilometres from the sea and, in County Antrim, further north, in a series of basalt cliffs punctuated by lonely valleys. From Antrim it is possible to see the Hebrides on a clear day; and from this proximity to Scotland derive, ultimately, all Northern Ireland's troubles.

During the early history of Scotland and Ireland, the Irish Sea acted not as a barrier but as a pool of Celtic and Christian cultures. After the Reformation, however, the links between the powerful, Catholic Highland leaders and their brothers by blood and religion in Ulster were seen as a threat to Protestant Britain. To forestall the menace of a Catholic confederacy, James I, first king of England and Scotland, took the drastic measure of settling Ulster with loyal Protestants, mainly from the Presbyterian Scottish Lowlands. By 1641, there were between 50,000 and 100,000 settlers established on Ulster "plantations". The native Catholic Irish were dispossessed of the best land, often with great violence, but allowed to remain on the worst and least cultivable parts of the plantations.

Thus a rift was opened not only between the British and the Irish, but also between the south of Ireland and the north, where the Protestants gained and kept a numerical ascendancy: in the 1980s, their population remains about 50 per cent higher than that of the Catholics. Economically, too, the development of Northern Ireland differed from the south. While the Industrial Revolution hardly touched the south, which then suffered from famine when crops failed, Northern Ireland

SELF-SUFFICIENCY IN THE SHETLANDS

Situated 200 kilometres north of Scotland, the isolated Shetland Islands have evolved and maintained a distinctive culture of their own. For centuries, islanders have won their livelihoods from fishing and from their crofts—smallholdings that provide grain and vegetables, peat for fuel and pasture for sheep. Shetland women have a long tradition of knitting, and Fair Isle, 40 kilometres south-west of the main island, has a worldwide reputation for its intricately patterned sweaters.

New wealth and industry came to the islands after oil was discovered in the North Sea east of the Shetlands in 1969. Today, the main island houses Europe's largest oil and liquefied gas terminal, and the oil business employs around a thousand of the 23,000 Shetlanders. The time-honoured occupations still flourish, however, and the islanders cling fiercely to their traditions.

Built just above the high tidemark, a typical Shetland croft allows easy access to the sea.

built an industrial economy around shipbuilding and linen manufacture.

The schism between Protestant, industrialized Ulster and the Catholic, rural south stimulated the Protestant majority in the North to resist any attempt by the British Parliament to make the province part of a united Ireland. In 1921, when the south gained Home Rule, Northern Ireland became an autonomous province of the United Kingdom. It had its own parliament which sat at Stormont Castle just outside Belfast, but Westminster retained responsibility for the province's defence and foreign policy, and remained the superior legislature, empowered to impose direct rule from London.

The 1921 settlement strengthened the Protestant ascendancy in the North. Catholics and Protestants were segregated in their housing, education and commerce, and preserved a kind of atavistic tribalism in secret organizations that commemorated long-past victories and humiliations. Stormont itself discriminated against the Catholic minority in school financing and employment; and it ensured that Catholics were not adequately represented in government by the gerrymandering of local government districts.

After 1965, the Northern Ireland prime minister, Captain Terence O'Neill, began to plan concessions to the Catholic community, but the projected reforms did little to appease the minority and, among the Protestants, only served to inflame their fears of a sell-out. In 1968, moderate Catholics campaigning for better housing were attacked by Protestants, including members of the police force; and in 1969 renewed Catholic demonstrations resulted in the first death of the campaign. At Northern Ireland's request, Westminster sent in troops to keep the peace. But disorder escalated. The Catholics were no longer campaigning for civil rights; spearheaded by the provisional wing of the Irish Republican Army—an illegal paramilitary organization based in the Republic of Ireland—they were fighting for nothing less than an Ireland united under the government of the Irish Republic.

Ironically, the troops sent in to protect the Catholics became the main target of the I.R.A. Alarmed by the breakdown of law and order, Westminster imposed direct rule on Northern Ireland in 1972. In response, the I.R.A. extended their terrorist activities to England. From 1969 to the end of 1985, the death toll was more than 2,400. Today Northern Ireland remains a

A crofting couple pack away slabs of peat—partially decomposed vegetable matter—which they have cut from a hillside. Fresh peat contains more than 90 per cent water and it must be dried for several weeks before it will burn.

A fisherman stands beside his catch of whiting, strung up on the croft wall to dry in the wind. The rich waters around the islands also yield mackerel, haddock and herring.

running sore on Britain's body politic. No end to the agony is in sight, since no proposal for the future of the province finds acceptance among Protestants and Catholics. All that has happened since direct rule is that a new generation has grown up in civil war with new sacrifices to celebrate and a new set of saints and devils to revere and hate.

During the 1970s—a decade of economic malaise throughout the United Kingdom—the events in Ireland seemed to infect Scotland and Wales, where nationalism arose to cast serious doubts on the cohesion of the nation. Since the Act of Union, nationalism had been virtually a dead issue in Scotland. The discovery of North Sea oil brought long-hidden resentments and aspirations to the surface. "It's Scotland's oil" became the slogan of the Scottish Nationalist Party; "if oil means something to 56 million Britons, it can mean ten times more to five million Scots." The SNP's campaign soon achieved results at the polls. In 1967, the SNP had one seat in Parliament. After the October 1974 General Election, in which they gained more than 30 per cent of the Scottish vote, the Nationalists carried 11 seats.

A similar surge in the nationalists' fortunes occurred in Wales, where three of the country's 36 seats were won by the Welsh nationalist party, Plaid Cymru, in October 1974. In Wales, which lacked both oil and Scotland's separate legal and religious institutions, the nationalist movement was devoted to reviving the Welsh language and culture—notably by pressing for the widest possible use of the language on TV, in the courts and in government publications. In both countries there was some violence, which in Wales took the form of burning weekend cot-

A little girl receives tuition in the tin whistle, one of the indispensable accompaniments to Irish folk music. Still very popular in Northern Ireland, traditional Irish music is also played in pubs and clubs in English cities that have Irish communities.

tages owned by non-Welsh families and destroying English road-signs.

The Labour government of 1974 had no overall majority and needed the support of the nationalist members to stay in power. Devolution was the price of that support. This union of political expediency and popular sentiment produced a sickly child: the Scotland and Wales Bill, which proposed a Scottish Assembly that could legislate for health, education, local government and law and order; and a Welsh Assembly that would take over some functions previously exercised by ministers in London, but would have no legislative powers whatsoever. There was one proviso, however: the measures would come into force only if a minimum of 40 per cent of the total electorate voted for the proposals in referenda. The referenda took place on March 1, 1979.

Wales voted against devolution. In Scotland, a small majority among those who turned out to vote wanted devolution but they did not add up to 40 per cent of the total electorate. So in both countries the proposals foun-

dered, and their proponents with them. After the General Election of 1983, only four nationalist members of Parliament remained at Westminster.

In the 1980s, nationalist sentiment in Wales continued to focus on language and culture. The former nationalist M.P. Gwynfor Evans won a fight in 1982 to have a TV channel broadcasting entirely in Welsh after he had threatened a fast to the death if the measure was refused. Political separatism, however, is virtually a dead issue.

In Scotland, demands for home rule did not altogether disappear with the devolution referendum, and there was lingering resentment at the way it had been organized. "Governments have been elected with smaller majorities," complained an Edinburgh teacher four years after the vote. Yet he was vague about the nature of a possible independent Scotland, admitting that the only vital difference between England and his own country was that "England has the power, and we don't". And away from the cities, it is difficult to find any strong desire for independence. EEC funds for underdeveloped rural regions have brought unprecedented prosperity to large areas of the Scottish countryside, and the Scottish Development Agency, which was set up after the devolution crisis, has blunted the worst effects of the recession.

So, as Britain thankfully turns its back on the constitutional traumas of the 1970s, the only serious threat to the unity of the kingdom is the ever-present spectre of Northern Ireland. Many problems remain—notably the growing economic gap between north and south, and the decay of the inner cities. Yet the devolution vote showed, if only feebly, that the diverse peoples of Britain prefer to face the future together.

IMAGES OF SECTARIAN STRIFE

William of Orange brandishes his sword.

Behind a bomb-shattered car, a Christ figure gazes compassionately down on a prisoner.

The sectarian rifts between Northern Ireland's Protestant and Catholic communities are prominently aired in the wall paintings that decorate the province's towns. While some commemorate historical victories, others make political points or vent grievances. The artists on both sides use religious symbols to arouse the sympathy of their supporters.

In Protestant areas, many of the paintings feature William of Orange, a Protestant Dutch prince who, at the invitation of the British Parliament, became Britain's King William III in 1688. In 1689 his ousted Catholic predecessor, James II, led a rebellion against him in Ireland, but William defeated James's Catholic forces at the Battle of the Boyne, near Dublin, in 1690. Pictures of William also adorn banners of the Orangemen, who take their name from their hero and who parade through Belfast on July 12 each year to celebrate his victory.

Many of the paintings in Catholic areas make propaganda out of the sufferings of terrorists convicted for taking part in the campaign to unite Northern Ireland with the republican south. The painting below, signed by a group opposed to the treatment of terrorists in Northern Ireland's prisons, includes a quotation from Bobby Sands, an activist in the illegal Irish Republican Army, who died in prison after a 66-day hunger strike.

Superimposed on the flag of the old united Ireland, a symbolic bird of peace struggles in barbed wire.

ASPECTS OF A CHERISHED COUNTRYSIDE

Within their narrow compass, the British Isles contain a marked variety of natural beauty. From the Celtic west, where uptilted rocks confront the Atlantic as towering cliffs, to the fertile eastern plain that grades imperceptibly into the shallow sea, from the windswept moors of Scotland to the lush, drowsy valleys of Dorset, there is a whole range of rural idylls to choose from, each with its own claim to be considered the quintessential Britain.

Almost all bear the mark of man—and therein lies much of their appeal. The generations of settlers and cultivators who smoothed hilltops, cleared forests, drained marshes and planted hedges have left the countryside strewn with evocative records of their endeavours. The man-made features of the landscape blend in gracefully, enhancing rather than detracting from nature's contribution.

Pervaded as it is with the life of their ancestors and the rhythms of nature, the countryside is to British people the true heart of the nation. But paradoxically it has long been unfamiliar territory to most of them. Industrialization came early to Britain and as long ago as 1851 more than half the population lived in towns and cities; today the figure is around 80 per cent. To those who see it but rarely, the countryside is all the more precious; its timeless loveliness never fails to delight and refresh the spirit.

Centuries of continuous use have etched the winding course of a narrow lane deeply into the face of the Devon countryside.

The wintry peak of Snowdon—at 1,085 metres the highest mountain in Wales—is reflected in the chill waters of a small lake.

The flat floor of the Langdale Valley has long offered a haven for habitation among the rugged hills of Cumbria in north-western England.

On the slopes leading to the bleak plateau of Dartmoor in Devon, Widecombe village lies embowered among trees.

Scattered stone barns punctuate the freshly mown pastureland in Yorkshire's Wensleydale, where the wide, shallow valleys were scooped out by prehistoric glaciation.

A cottage built of the local golden limestone overlooks the glassy surface of the River Windrush in the Cotswold hills of Gloucestershire.

On the island of Lewis in the Outer Hebrides, off the west coast of Scotland, the harsh land dictates the pattern of settlement. Each household in the farming and fishing community has its share of the narrow coastal slope of grazing land; behind the houses lie the barren uplands of the island's interior, in front of them an inlet of the sea.

Ancient rocks worn smooth by the sea
rise above a sandy bay on Scotland's
east coast. Along the shore south of
Aberdeen, unspoilt beaches alternate
with precipitous cliffs and salt-flats.

Resembling an intricate tessellated pavement, the Giant's Causeway on the coast of County Antrim is composed of volcanic basalt that split into huge hexagonal prisms as it cooled more than 30 million years ago.

2

longtain voyage: quil souffra de porter seulemet vng
las de soye a vng ymage de saint george pendat a icellui.
Aussi se ledit colier dor auoit besoing de reparacion il poia
estre mis en la main de louurier iusques a ce quil soit
repure. Lequel colier aussi ne pourra estre enrichy de
pierres ou daultres choses reserue les ymage qui pourra
estre garny au plaisir du cheualier. Et aussi ne pourra
estre ledit colier vendu engaige donne ne aliene pour
necessite ou cause quelconque que ce soit

In a 16th-century illustration, Edward
I (1239–1307) presides over an early
Parliament. The rulers of Scotland and
Wales—who in reality did not attend
the Parliament—symbolize Edward's
ambition to dominate Britain. The text
describes the Order of the Garter,
established in 1348 by Edward III.

INSTITUTIONS THAT ENDURE

It is, as one would expect from the British, a magnificent spectacle. Her Majesty, Queen Elizabeth II, by the grace of God Sovereign of the United Kingdom of Great Britain and Northern Ireland, Head of the Commonwealth and Defender of the Faith, drives in great pomp from Buckingham Palace to Westminster, there to inaugurate the session of her loyal Parliament of Lords and Commons. In the baroque splendour of her gilded State Coach, amid a jingling escort of her Household Cavalry in bobbing plumes and gleaming breastplates, she passes along the superb avenue of the Mall. Behind a line of red-coated guardsmen, her people cheer her.

At her Palace of Westminster—to give the parliament buildings their formal title—the Queen is received by the Officers of State; the whole glittering procession then makes its way to the chamber of the House of Lords where the peers of the realm, gloriously attired in scarlet and ermine, arise to greet her. She bids them be seated; at her command, the Gentleman Usher of the Black Rod—an officer who is vested with the largely ceremonial task of keeping order in the House—sets off to the adjacent House of Commons to summon its members to the royal presence. There, for his pains, the door to the chamber is solemnly slammed in his face: the Commons are asserting their hard-won right to keep out the Crown and its servants. Only after Black Rod has knocked politely three times is he allowed to enter and convey his message, whereupon the Commons,

their point made, troop off to the House of Lords with a good grace.

The purpose of the ceremony is now made apparent. The Lord Chancellor, the highest law official in the land, kneels before the throne and presents to Her Majesty a speech that she proceeds to read. In clear but neutral tones, she outlines the policy of her government and the legislation that it plans in the forthcoming parliamentary session.

Her neutral voice is imposed by constitutional convention, but is natural in any case since not one word of the speech is her own. It has been written for her by the Cabinet—the group of 20 or so senior ministers who initiate legislation and control the various areas of government—and Her Majesty will not deviate from it by so much as a comma. For the Queen's Speech to Parliament is not an exercise of royal power, as appearances might suggest, but a symbol of the taming of the monarchy. Once, the monarch could summon his Parliament wherever and whenever he pleased, and tell it whatever he chose. Today, the royal authority is vestigial; and power has passed from the sumptuously attired Lords to the sober-suited gentlemen of the Commons who, when the Queen's Speech is completed, will retire to the security of their chamber where they could, if they pleased, tear the government's policy to shreds were it not for the fact that the government normally commands the allegiance of a majority of the members of Parliament.

In England, democratic forms of government and the rule of law can be

traced back in an unbroken line to medieval times. That, at least, is what British schoolchildren are taught, and in a sense it is true. Democratic institutions of a sort did exist 900 years ago and, though they all but lost their strength in Renaissance England, a thread of continuity does link them with the present day. But it is not the antiquity of their political forms that distinguishes the British so much as the remarkable way in which they have, with a minimum of violence, adapted the basic fabric of monarchy and parliament to the needs of different ages.

Unlike most states, Britain has no written constitution. This omission, rather than hampering the growth of democracy, has been an asset. In contrast with other, written, constitutions, that of Britain is self-amending: conventions, precedents, legal strictures and safeguards abound, but up to a point an action is constitutional if it is acceptable to the nation—that is, if the government can get away with it. In times of unrest, Britain's rulers have almost always chosen to bend with the wind rather than be destroyed by the gale—to accept a curtailing of their powers or an extension of the franchise—and the constitution has usually permitted the necessary manoeuvring.

There is really no fixed point in British history from which constitutional government—in the sense of the legal regulation and the sharing of power—can be said to begin. With a little historical licence, the idea can be traced back to the witan, the assembly of wise men

who advised the Saxon kings. As a coherent and continuing development, though, it originated in the years after the Norman Conquest of 1066.

When William of Normandy seized the realm of England, he appropriated all land and allocated huge tracts to his barons in return for their homage and military service. Since the barons held the land only as the king's gift, his authority seemed unchallengeable. But unfortunately for William's successors, many of the barons became immensely powerful in their localities. They could not be counted on to stay loyal, and to assure popular support against the aristocracy, many an English king was obliged to restrict his own absolute power by promising the people a rule based on law and justice. With the help of the people, he could restrain his barons; with the barons safely in hand, he could renege on his promise and oppress the people to his heart's content.

Such a policy demanded only modest skill, since it was difficult to outrage every section of society at the same time. That feat, however, was accomplished in the 13th century by King John. John waged expensive wars on the Continent and imposed heavy taxes to pay for them, thus angering the barons and the merchants on whom the taxes fell. He also deeply offended the Church by conducting a long-drawn-out quarrel with Pope Innocent III (which John lost) over who should appoint the nation's primate, the Archbishop of Canterbury. In 1215 the barons, merchants and clergy—the most powerful elements of English society—formed a coalition against the King. Virtually at swordpoint, the monarch assented to a document that was to be the foundation stone of the British constitution: the Magna Carta.

In essence, the Great Charter set out legal ground rules for kingship, re-

Pharaoh in the guise of an Anglo-Saxon king with his witan, or council, of wise men illustrates an 11th-century Old Testament manuscript. The witan remained the chief instrument of English government until the Norman conquest of 1066.

stricting the arbitrary use of power and allowing taxation only with the consent of a Great Council of the Realm. Significantly, it included a clause explicitly doubting the monarch's willingness to stick to his bargain, and providing for armed coercion if he did not.

The Magna Carta has long been enshrined in the mythology of the English-speaking democracies; during the 1976 U.S. bicentennial celebrations, 10 million Americans viewed one of the four surviving original documents, lent by the British for the occasion. It is certainly easy to exaggerate Magna Carta's importance as the fountainhead of liberty. Most of the rights were restricted to the baronage, and the common people, both rich or poor, gained little or nothing. Its real significance lay in the future: in time, claims for privileges set out in its clauses could be translated into the universal language of freedom and justice.

King John repudiated Magna Carta almost immediately, as his subjects had foreseen, but it did him little good: he died the next year and subsequent kings summoned their Great Councils—which soon came to be known as Parliaments—when they needed extra taxes. At first the councils were composed exclusively of barons and churchmen, but from 1265 onwards some included knights from each shire and commoners from the towns. By 1327 Parliament was actually strong enough to depose a king—Edward II—and replace him with his young son, Edward III. Ten years later, the Hundred Years War with France began, and Edward III's constant need for money to wage it enhanced Parliament's power still further.

In this period, the institution took on something similar to its modern form.

In a Somerset church, a 14th-century stained glass fragment commemorates Sir Thomas Hungerford, a local landowner who in 1377 became the first presiding officer of the House of Commons to be designated "Speaker of the House"—a title that survives today.

The Commons, the knights and townsmen, began to sit separately from the clergy and the barons, who made up what would eventually become the House of Lords. The Commons rapidly increased in self-confidence, and in 1376 its presiding officer was bold enough to demand the impeachment of corrupt and incompetent royal ministers as well as the right to inspect the national accounts and numerous other constitutional changes. Two ministers were duly impeached and condemned before the Lords. But before the Commons had proceeded much further in its work of reform, John of Gaunt, the fourth son of the ageing King Edward III and the dominant figure at court, resolved to restore the collapsing prestige of the king. He annulled the acts of the Good Parliament and threw the presiding officer into prison.

The medieval Parliament never again matched the achievements of the heady days of 1376. Parliament was only one of many competing forces in the kingdom, and in the 15th century the end of the war with France, and the concomitant reduction in expenditure, lessened the king's financial dependence on it. Then, in 1455, only two

years after hostilities with France had ended, a murderous 30-year dynastic struggle for the throne of England began. The Wars of the Roses—so named by Sir Walter Scott because the emblems of the opposing factions were a red and a white rose respectively—obliterated the nation's slowly developing civil liberties. When the dust settled towards the end of the century, the new king, Henry VII, held the government of the country more firmly in his hands than had any monarch since William the Conqueror. Huge confiscations of wealth and land from the war's losers liberated him from the need to summon Parliaments. The old baronage was dead or in disarray; and the Commons had been reduced to a fearful cipher.

This was the kingdom inherited by Henry VIII in 1509: an unchallenged autocracy with a well-filled treasury. The realm of England was well on the way, apparently, to becoming an absolute monarchy along the pattern then developing elsewhere in Europe. That it did not do so was due to a unique combination of factors. The first was Henry's expensive foreign policy, which included warring with France and Scotland. The fighting obliged the King to levy heavy taxes and returned to Parliament some measure of budgetary control.

The second, and most dramatic, was Henry's determination to divorce his first wife, against the wishes of the Pope. The ideas of the Protestant Reformation were beginning to sweep Europe, so that Henry found plenty of support for the independent Church of England he had resolved to establish in order to evade the Pope's veto on his divorce. Between 1529 and 1536, Parliament, at Henry's instigation, passed statutes sweeping away the power of

47

2

the papacy in England and vesting it in the Crown instead. As head of the new Church, Henry dissolved the nation's ancient monasteries, which at one stroke satisfied Protestant principles and liberated for royal use the enormous wealth of these foundations. He got his divorce, of course—indeed, he went on to have six wives in all. But he also relinquished some of his authority. Parliament had been strengthened by its central role in the great religious change. Moreover, the English Reformation which Henry began encouraged a tradition of independent thinking that fitted ill with the ideas of authoritarian kingship. Freed from papal authority—its principal tie to continental Europe—Britain was able to develop its own political institutions in its own idiosyncratic way.

The third factor that sent Britain on a different political course from its continental neighbours was the changed social organization of a nation fast evolving out of the Middle Ages. The changes were already discernible in Henry VIII's time, but had become more apparent by the reign of his daughter Queen Elizabeth I in the late 16th century. The population was expanding and finding employment in an increasingly wide range of industries. Trade in wool and woollen cloth had brought unprecedented wealth to many parts of the country; mining, steel-making, printing and paper-making were also becoming important. Towns prospered and they jealously guarded rights that were often confirmed by royal charters. The old feudal aristocracy had largely vanished, and it was replaced by a new class of country gentlemen who made themselves responsible for the day-to-day administration outside the capital,

serving as unpaid magistrates and also regularly electing each other as members of the House of Commons.

The increasingly outspoken debates of that body rarely inconvenienced Elizabeth: throughout her reign the royal prerogatives remained unchallenged. But she was a hugely popular monarch, who had led her country to victory in a dangerous war with Spain; her successor James I had no such advantage. James, ruler of England and Scotland, spent most of his reign at loggerheads with an English Parliament increas-

ingly inclined to assert its political authority over questions of taxation, religion and foreign policy.

When James's son Charles I came to the throne in 1625, he was as determined as his father to exercise what he saw as his God-given rights to kingship. But Parliament, on its side, had set itself to dismantle royal autocracy. The Parliament of 1640–1641 declared it illegal for the monarch to collect taxes without parliamentary sanction, and voted to abolish courts in which the king or his councillors judged cases

Henry VIII sits bestride a prostrate Pope Clement VII in an allegorical woodcut that celebrates the King's appropriation of authority over the English church in the 1530s. By the King's side stand the two instruments of his breach with Rome—Archbishop Cranmer and Thomas Cromwell.

directly and without appeal. Charles agreed to the reforms with great reluctance and he looked for the first opportunity for retracting his consent. A showdown became inescapable.

As if the political conflicts were not enough, the situation was exacerbated by the tendency of the Commons to the extreme Puritan forms of Protestantism and of the court towards the old Catholic faith. (Charles did in fact adhere to the Church of England, but his queen was a Catholic.) In October 1641, the Catholics in Ireland rebelled against Protestant rule. Parliament suspected—mistakenly, as it happened—that the Irish revolt was a move in a counter-revolutionary plot of the King's. Troops were urgently needed to restore order; the King, by ancient tradition, would control the army that was raised and appoint its head. An influential section of Parliament, fearing the power of the King once he had troops at his call, refused to trust a royal nominee with command of any army. With passions aroused by the Irish crisis, the House of Commons then debated and passed a comprehensive indictment of royal policy and set forth proposals for a thorough reform of the Church. Charles reacted to the challenges to his authority by bursting into the House of Commons with a body of armed men and attempting to arrest five members of Parliament for treason. They eluded him, however, and escaped by boat. In the ensuing weeks, the country began to take sides with the King or with Parliament, and in 1642 civil war broke out. It was the greatest upheaval in English history.

After four years of fighting, Parliament, in the shape of the most militant section of the House of Commons, achieved total victory. In 1649, King Charles was beheaded as an enemy of the people, the House of Lords was abolished and Oliver Cromwell, an obscure member of Parliament who had risen to power at the head of the huge army Parliament had created, became virtual dictator.

Such an outcome was not what the country squires and the prosperous burghers who first opposed the King had had in mind. To make things worse, the psalm-singing soldiers of the new army, encouraged by fundamentalist Protestant preachers, were demanding a real social revolution. "Babylon has fallen" was the cry; and those whose pikes had pushed it down wanted a fair share of the theocratic republic they expected to replace it. Cromwell, though, was more a country gentleman than a revolutionary. The army's demagogues were imprisoned or shot; and the most alarmingly democratic of the many Protestant sects were put down. Cromwell established a "Commonwealth" with himself as Lord Protector, but though he was feared he was never loved and the Commonwealth virtually died with him in 1658. Two years later, the landed gentry and the well-off urban middle classes who between them now ran the country restored the House of Lords and invited the son of their executed king to return from exile as Charles II.

It was a bizarre choice, but a wise one—at least as far as peace and quiet were concerned. Most of the population had had enough of military rule; Puritan morality had become equally tiresome. Charles for his part agreed to the surrender of many of the royal prerogatives his father had fought for: special royal courts, for instance, now vanished never to return, and the King himself was bound by the Common Law of England. Generally, he was prepared to be conciliatory: he did not want, he said, to go on his travels again.

His brother, James II, was less compromising. In a nation by now thoroughly Protestant, he was an ardent Roman Catholic, and determined to subject Church and country to his faith. In furthering his aims he openly defied the laws of the land, and attacked a number of powerful vested interests—not only the Church but also the universities and the municipal authorities. It became clear to his subjects that if his reign were allowed to continue it would simply set the clock back 50 years or more. United for once, every social class in the country shuddered at the thought, and James suffered the most ignominious fate that can befall a king: he was sacked by his own people. Without undue fuss, a Convention Parliament then summoned itself and, suspicious of republics, invited James's reliably Protestant daughter Mary and her Dutch husband, William of Orange, to assume the throne. James fled the country and took refuge at the court of France.

The event went down in British history as the Glorious Revolution of 1688—rightly so. Without the savagery of a civil war, the British constitution was transformed adroitly into some-

49

thing like its modern form. By the Bill of Rights, cheerfully assented to by the new monarchs much as a worker signs a contract of employment, the supremacy of Parliament over the throne was absolutely secured.

The Bill of Rights abolished the monarch's power to suspend Parliament and made Parliament's approval vital if a standing army was to be raised in peacetime. It established the succession—giving the throne to William and Mary jointly and on their deaths to Mary's sister Anne. It also specifically barred Catholics from the throne. In a sense this last clause was the most crucial, for implied in it was the legislators' conviction that kingship could not be unconditional. Government, in their eyes, was a social contract between the king and his people, who were represented by Parliament, and if the king did not fulfil his side of the bargain his people had no moral obligation to tolerate him. A new form of Coronation oath left no doubt about the relationship: the monarch had to promise to "govern according to the statutes in Parliament agreed on".

During the reign of William and Mary, Parliament developed the most powerful weapon it had to control the monarchy—finance. In previous reigns the Crown could depend partly on hereditary revenues, but these now amounted to very little. Parliament granted the monarch an annual sum to cover the cost of the court and civil government, and any additional expenditure had to be debated and carried on its own merits. With the money available to him, the king no longer had the slightest chance of making himself independent of Parliament or of maintaining an army against its will.

The 17th century saw England diverge sharply from the constitutional practices of continental Europe. Up to this period, its embryonic democratic institutions had been matched by counterparts elsewhere. But by the 1800s, France, Prussia, Austria, Hungary and Bohemia, Spain, Italy and the Netherlands had all fallen under absolute rule; for them, this was the age of despotic kings and emperors. England, by contrast, remembers this period as the age when Parliament reached maturity and successfully challenged the authority of monarchs—first in the Civil War, later and decisively with the Glorious Revolution. Having set limits to autocratic

RE-FIGHTING OLD BATTLES

The British have a keen appetite for history and the country proliferates with societies dedicated to re-creating the events of bygone days—from medieval jousting tournaments to the battles against Napoleon in the early 19th century.

One such organization is the Sealed Knot, which restages the Civil War battles fought in the 1640s between the Cavaliers—the supporters of King Charles I—and the forces of Parliament, known as Roundheads. Named after a group loyal to the King, the Sealed Knot of today can field some 5,000 members armed with pikes and halberds. To make each clash as authentic as possible, they fight on the sites of the original battles, or at places with appropriate historical associations.

Present-day Royalists and Parliamentarians clash amid the smoke from fired muskets.

DIT HVYS IS TE HEER.

THIS HOVSE IS TO LETE

Be gone you rogues
You haue Sate long enough

C: Cuper

C: Lau:

G. O: Cromwel.

This is an Oule.

rule so early in its history, Britain has ever since escaped internal convulsions. As the Victorian historian Lord Macaulay put it: "because we had a preserving revolution in the 17th century... we have not had a destroying revolution in the 19th century."

Although the House of Commons achieved so much in the 17th century, it adapted itself only slowly to its new responsibilities. As an institution, it had evolved largely as a force of opposition rather than a source of policy, and for much of the 18th century policy remained the king's prerogative, exercised with the aid of his ministers.

After the Bill of Rights, however, it became essential for the king's ministers to command a majority in Parliament and in this they were sometimes helped, sometimes hindered by the appearance on the scene of political parties. Whigs—in general, opponents of royal power—and Tories—in general supporters of it—came into being in the late 17th century. Interestingly, both names were originally terms of abuse devised by opponents; more interestingly still, both parties have continued in a more-or-less unbroken line

to the present day, the Whigs becoming the Liberal Party and the Tories the Conservatives. For 250 years the two factions jockeyed for power; the fact that neither was ever able to achieve a permanent monopoly of it was the greatest guarantee of the continuing development of British civil liberties.

Gradually, policy-making shifted from the king to his ministers. In the first half of the 18th century, it became the convention that ministers should be drawn exclusively from Parliament, and chiefly from the Commons. By the mid-18th century, one of the important

A CHRONOLOGY OF KEY EVENTS

c. 200,000 B.C. Stone Age hunters begin to move freely in and out of Britain, which at this time forms part of the continental landmass.

6000–5000 B.C. Great Britain becomes an island, cut off from the European mainland by the English Channel.

c. 4000 B.C. New Stone Age immigrants from Europe introduce farming to Britain.

c. 2000 B.C. The Bronze Age arrives with the invasion of peoples from the Rhine basin. They build Stonehenge, a sacred circle of monumental stones in Wiltshire.

700–100 B.C. Celtic tribes from central Europe invade and introduce the use of iron to Britain.

55–54 B.C. Julius Caesar makes two expeditions to Britain and names the island "Britannia".

43–c. 407 A.D. The Romans invade and quickly overrun the English and Welsh lowlands. They invade Scotland but fail to hold it. Four centuries of occupation follow, but by the start of the fifth century, the Roman Empire is in decline and Roman troops are withdrawn from Britain.

c. 400 Armed Saxon warriors from northern Europe *(helmet, below)* harry and eventually conquer England.

563–664 Christianity gains ground in Great Britain. In 563, the Irish evangelist St. Columba founds a monastery in western Scotland. In 597, St. Augustine from Rome converts the Saxons in Kent. For decades, Irish and

Roman missions contend for control of the Church. In 664, the Synod of Whitby decides in favour of the Roman Church.

793 Vikings from Scandinavia sack the great monastery on Lindisfarne, an island off the coast of Northumbria. Other raids follow but later the Vikings settle peacefully. In 1016, the Danish King Canute becomes king of all England and part of Scotland.

1066 William, Duke of Normandy, leads the last invasion of England and defeats the English at the Battle of Hastings. He is crowned William I, the first of the Norman dynasty.

1106–1135 Henry I takes Normandy from his brother Robert, establishing England's first foothold in France.

1154–1189 Henry II, first of the Plantagenet dynasty, rules England in a time of peace and prosperity. Legal reforms give the whole population access to the king's central courts. From precedents set in these courts, the English system of Common Law develops. Thomas à Becket is assassinated by four of Henry's knights in 1170 in Canterbury Cathedral after resisting Henry's attempts to reduce the power of the Church. This marks the beginning of Crown opposition to the Church of Rome.

1215 King John's demands for high taxes to pay for unsuccessful wars with France enrage the barons, who force John to assent *(right)* to Magna Carta—a document designed to safeguard the barons' rights and to prevent misuse of power by the king.

1249–1284 The first colleges are founded at Oxford and Cambridge.

1264 Once more in conflict with their king over taxation, the barons, led by Simon de Montfort, take to arms and defeat Henry III at Lewes. In 1265, de Montfort summons a short-lived Parliament composed of both knights and commoners from the towns.

1272–1307 Edward I conquers Wales and makes war with Scotland. In order to raise money for the Scottish wars, Edward summons the Model Parliament, which represents all three estates of the realm—clergy, nobles and commons.

1314 Scotland retains independence with the defeat of Edward II's army at the Battle of Bannockburn.

1337–1455 England's aspirations for an empire in France bring about the Hundred Years War. Some notable victories give England control, for a spell, of large parts of western France. The girl-soldier Joan of Arc kindles a spirit of resistance in her French compatriots; by 1453 the French have regained all but Calais.

1348–1349 The bubonic plague or Black Death reduces the population by a third.

1455–1485 The so-called "Wars of the Roses" are fought between the houses of York and Lancaster as each claims the throne. Neither gains the long-term

advantage: in 1485, Henry Tudor wins the battle of Bosworth Field and is crowned Henry VII. His dynasty reigns until 1603.

1529–1536 The Reformation Parliament supports Henry VIII in breaking with the Church of Rome. Henry is recognized as Supreme Head of the Church of England.

1553 Mary Tudor succeeds to the throne. She restores Catholicism as the official religion.

1558–1603 Elizabeth I re-establishes the Church of England. Under her glorious rule, Britain emerges as a great European power. Commerce and industry prosper and some of Britain's greatest literature is written.

1577–1580 Francis Drake *(below)* circumnavigates the globe.

1588 The defeat of the Spanish Armada prevents an invasion and opens an era of British naval supremacy.

1600 The East India Company begins trading in the Indian seas.

1603 James Stuart is the first king to rule England and Scotland as James VI in Scotland and James I in England.

1607 The first English settlement in North America is founded in Virginia.

1625 Charles I succeeds to the throne. Fierce conflict between Charles and Parliament over the extent of the monarch's power marks his reign.

1642–1646 The English Civil War is fought between the armies of the King and Parliament. The Parliamentarians, under Oliver Cromwell, are victorious.

1649 Charles I is beheaded, the monarchy and House of Lords are abolished and a republic is formed under Oliver Cromwell.

1660 Soon after Cromwell's death, Parliament offers the throne to Charles I's son. He is crowned Charles II.

1668 Isaac Newton, the father of modern physics, experiments with light and constructs the first reflecting telescope *(right)*.

1685 James II, a Roman Catholic, succeeds Charles II. He tries to impose his religion on the country.

1688–1689 The "Glorious Revolution" takes place against the Catholic monarch James II. Parliament invites William and Mary of Orange to ascend the throne—on Parliament's terms.

1707 The Treaty of Union, adopted by both the English and the Scottish Parliaments, joins England and Scotland under the name of Great Britain.

1700–1800 Great advances are made in agriculture: proper drainage, better strains of wheat, selective breeding of stock, and crop rotation all contribute to more efficient farming.

1714–1727 George I reigns.

1727 George II succeeds George I.

1760 George III succeeds George II.

1765 James Watt develops a commercially viable engine that harnesses steam power.

1769 Richard Arkwright patents the water-frame, a mechanized spinning device which makes mass production of thread possible.

1775 The American War of Independence breaks out after Britain tries to impose taxes on the colonies. In 1783, after defeat in battle, Britain recognizes the United States of America.

1793 Britain declares war on France after the French, under the revolutionary Directory, advance into the Netherlands. The war continues after 1799 when Napoleon comes to power.

1801 Great Britain and Ireland are joined to form the United Kingdom.

1805 Admiral Nelson defeats the French navy at the Battle of Trafalgar.

1815 The British Army under the Duke of Wellington defeats Napoleon's troops at the decisive Battle of Waterloo. The British and the other nations victorious against Napoleon settle the new frontiers of Europe at the Congress of Vienna.

1820 George IV succeeds George III.

1825–1855 Britain experiences the world's first railway boom *(below)*, and 13,000 kilometres of track are laid.

1830 William IV succeeds George IV.

1833 A Factory Act sets the minimum working age at nine years. Other reforms of working conditions in mines and factories soon follow.

1837–1901 Under Queen Victoria the British Empire expands to become "the empire on which the sun never sets".

1853 David Livingstone begins a three-year expedition through uncharted Central Africa.

1857 A rebellion in the Bengal army sparks off the Indian Mutiny, a popular

revolt against British rule in which thousands die. The Government of India Act of 1858 transfers administrative power in India from the East India Company to the Crown.

1859 Charles Darwin's *Origin of Species* is published. Darwin presents the evidence for the mutability of species and for their evolution, by natural selection, from a common ancestor.

1875 Britain acquires shares in the Suez Canal, thus safeguarding the route to India.

1877 Queen Victoria is proclaimed Empress of India.

1899–1902 The Boer War *(commemorated on a fan, below)* is fought in South Africa against settlers of Dutch descent. It gives Britain control of the Transvaal and Orange Free State but at a cost of 22,000 British lives.

1901–1910 Edward VII reigns.

1905–1911 Liberal governments institute important social reforms.

Old age pensions are introduced, health and unemployment insurance begun and labour exchanges established.

1910 George V succeeds Edward VII.

1914–1918 Imperialistic and economic rivalry between the European powers causes World War I. Aided by the late entry of the U.S., Britain and France emerge victorious over Germany.

1921 After violent clashes between Irish republicans and the authorities, independence is granted to southern Ireland, which becomes the Irish Free State (renamed Eire in 1937). Northern Ireland (Ulster) remains part of the United Kingdom.

1922 The British Broadcasting Company is founded. In 1927, it becomes a public Corporation.

1926 A miners' dispute over wages and hours leads to a General Strike, supported by most trade union members. Forewarned, the government prepares emergency measures. The strike is called off after nine days and in 1927, the Trades Dispute Act makes sympathetic strikes illegal.

1936 Edward VIII abdicates to marry Wallis Simpson, a twice-divorced American. His brother, the Duke of York, is crowned George VI.

1939 World War II begins. Britain declares war on Germany after Germany invades Poland.

1940 A coalition government is formed in May under Winston Churchill *(right, above)*. Three months later, the German airforce attempts to gain air superiority over the English Channel in preparation for an invasion of Britain. The British airforce confronts and overwhelms the German fighters in the Battle of Britain.

1944 On June 6, "D Day", thousands of Allied troops land on the Normandy beaches and advance against the German army.

1944 An Education Act reorganizes secondary schooling and makes it compulsory to age 15.

1945 World War II ends.

1945–1951 A Labour government nationalizes key industries and services: the Bank of England, railways, mines, steel, shipbuilding, gas and electricity. The National Health Service is instituted to extend free medical treatment to all. The National Assistance Act provides a weekly subsidy for those most in need.

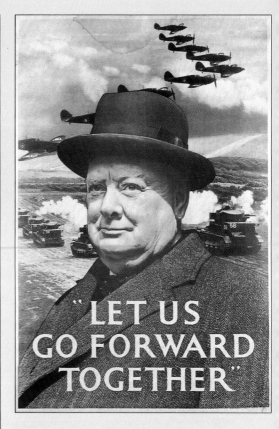

1947 The dissolution of the British Empire begins. India is given independence and the subcontinent is partitioned into India (Hindu) and Pakistan (Muslim).

1952 Elizabeth II succeeds to the throne.

1956 The Suez Crisis develops when the Egyptian leader Gamal Nasser nationalizes the Suez Canal, in which Britain has a controlling interest. Britain takes military action but backs down when the United Nations calls for an end to hostilities.

1968 Tension between Protestants and Catholics in Northern Ireland develops into near-civil war. At the request of the Northern Ireland government, British troops are sent in to keep the peace.

1969 Oil is discovered in the North Sea.

1973 Britain becomes a member of the European Economic Community.

1979 Margaret Thatcher, leader of the Conservative Party, becomes Britain's first woman prime minister.

features of modern British government had developed: the custom of ministers accepting collective responsibility for their government's actions. Policy was decided, as it still is, in private meetings during which there could be much dissension, but afterwards, in public, ministers presented a united front. Another crucial element of parliamentary rule also dates from this time; Sir Robert Walpole, who headed a Whig government from 1721 to 1742, is generally regarded as Britain's first prime minister, acting as leader both of the government and the Commons. There also emerged the beginnings of a modern civil service, in the shape of the increasing number of Treasury officials who handled day-to-day administration on behalf of the government.

By the end of the century, in fact, most of the modern British constitution was in existence, with one important exception—democracy. The House of Commons had always derived its legitimacy from its claim to represent the people; by 1800, that claim was looking very thin indeed. Even by the standards of the time, most elections were outrageously corrupt, and in many cases members of Parliament were virtually nominated by aristocratic landlords. The franchise was anomalous and highly restricted: in the country, only substantial property owners had the vote and many large towns, including Birmingham and Manchester, had no representation. Few politicians dreamt of granting voting rights to the common people, but the more perceptive were worried by the complete exclusion from the political process of the new middle classes who had risen to affluence with the Industrial Revolution.

The great Reform Act of 1832 eliminated the abuses and extended the

franchise—not to the British people as a whole, but at least to those of them who had enough money to be taken seriously by the government. This timely measure saved the British from the revolutions that plagued Europe in 1848. It also ensured the supreme authority of the Commons, because now its composition could be claimed truly to represent the people. Thenceforth, the fate of ministries was generally decided by elections, not by wheeling and dealing in Parliament, and the House of Lords occupied a progressively subordinate place in British politics.

As the century continued, and control of the government oscillated between Liberals and Conservatives, the franchise was steadily extended. Parties became increasingly organized. Electors paid more attention to candi-

dates' parties than their personalities; they voted, in effect, for the leaders of the parties. As a result, prime ministers could claim greater legitimacy and thus greater power than ever before. The constitution, as it operates today, was almost complete.

In the 20th century, there have been few formal changes. The House of Lords, hobbled in the 19th century by political convention, has been tethered more firmly still. The worst the Lords can do to Commons legislation is to delay it for a year, and over financial bills they have no veto whatsoever. The right to vote is now held by every British citizen from the age of 18, with the exception of criminals, lunatics and peers of the realm—who, since they have the right to sit in the House of Lords in person, are considered not to

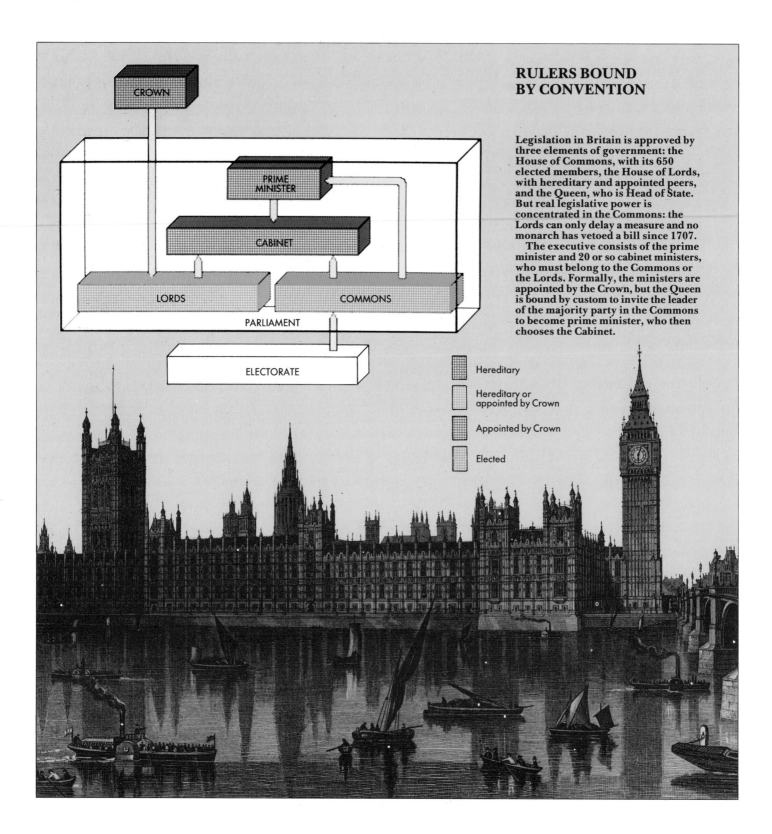

2

RULERS BOUND
BY CONVENTION

Legislation in Britain is approved by three elements of government: the House of Commons, with its 650 elected members, the House of Lords, with hereditary and appointed peers, and the Queen, who is Head of State. But real legislative power is concentrated in the Commons: the Lords can only delay a measure and no monarch has vetoed a bill since 1707.

The executive consists of the prime minister and 20 or so cabinet ministers, who must belong to the Commons or the Lords. Formally, the ministers are appointed by the Crown, but the Queen is bound by custom to invite the leader of the majority party in the Commons to become prime minister, who then chooses the Cabinet.

CROWN

PRIME
MINISTER

CABINET

LORDS

COMMONS

PARLIAMENT

ELECTORATE

Hereditary

Hereditary or
appointed by Crown

Appointed by Crown

Elected

In a cartoon of 1876, Prime Minister Benjamin Disraeli, in oriental attire, tempts Queen Victoria to assume the title "Empress of India". Disraeli's prime motive may have been to flatter the Queen, but his achievement was to strengthen both monarchy and Empire.

need indirect representation in the House of Commons.

Party loyalties have shifted, however. From the 1890s, more and more working-class voters turned to the new, socialist Labour Party; the Liberals in consequence declined, and the alternating two-party pattern continued. For a long time both parties supported the tacit consensus such a system required: the Labour Party was seldom as socialist as its rhetoric suggested, and the Conservatives—still, after three centuries, known as the Tories—were seldom as reactionary.

In the mid-1960s, Britain's increasingly acute economic problems began severely to weaken the consensus. The Labour Party and the Conservative Party both moved to more extreme positions, and incoming governments spent much parliamentary time undoing the work of their predecessors. Disillusioned by the spectacle, voters in the 1970s abandoned the two traditional parties by the million. Scottish and Welsh National Parties flowered briefly, and the Liberals, almost extinct for decades, became a major third force. In 1951, 97 per cent of the voters had opted for one of the two main parties; by the 1974 election, the percentage had fallen to 75 per cent. In 1981, a new Social Democratic Party broke away from Labour; the alliance it quickly formed with the Liberals was able to poll a quarter of the votes cast in the 1983 General Election.

The new, eclectic voting habits of the British are unlikely to herald an end of the familiar two-party sequence, however, for Britain has an electoral system that weighs heavily against third parties. At general elections (which take place at intervals of no more than five years), the 650 victors who will become members of Parliament need not obtain an absolute majority of the votes cast in their constituencies: Britain has a non-proportional, winner-take-all electoral system, which means that a plurality is quite sufficient. Thus it is perfectly possible to win a seat with far fewer votes than one's combined opponents. When there are only two parties in the contest, the result is usually reasonably fair; but when three parties are involved, the disproportion between the national tally of votes cast and the number of parliamentary seats won can be startling. In 1983, for instance, the Conservatives took 42 per cent of the vote, Labour 27 per cent and the new Alliance 25 per cent. Yet the Alliance won only 23 seats, while Labour gained 209 and the Conservatives scooped the pool with 397 seats.

In the British system, it is parliamentary seats that count. In constitutional practice, the leader of the party commanding a majority in the House of Commons when all the votes have been counted is summoned to Buckingham Palace by the monarch, and invited to form a government. The prime minister—for that is what he or she has now become—nominates the group of senior ministers, each responsible for a great department of state, who form the Cabinet. Most of them are members of the House of Commons; a few have

SNUFF AND CEREMONY AT WESTMINSTER

Everything about the Houses of Parliament speaks of the antiquity of British government institutions. The Commons and Lords have met on the same site for more than 400 years, and although the original 14th-century royal Palace of Westminster was destroyed by fire, its Victorian successor was built in a style that exuberantly recalls the Middle Ages. Many of the customs enacted within its walls are centuries old.

Each peer, for example, is greeted outside the House of Lords by a top-hatted attendant known as Red Coat, whose office goes back to the 17th century. In the House of Commons, another historic figure, the Principal Doorkeeper, bars the way to unauthorized persons and hands out snuff to any member who desires it. The Vote Office and the Printed Paper Office have been in existence for more than 200 years to provide members of Parliament and peers respectively with all the documents they may need for each day's sitting. And while the House of Commons library boasts computer links worldwide, members living within 5 kilometres of Westminster still have papers hand-delivered by messengers known as "walkmen".

In the traceried cloakroom, each peer has his own coat hook.

A gothic calendar and stationery holder grace a library desk.

Stone arches frame the Vote Office.

Red Coat awaits their Lordships.

Tapestries line the Lords' dining room.

seats in the Lords, but none come from outside Parliament.

During the forthcoming parliamentary session, the government introduces legislation before the House. In theory, the members debate new bills according to their merits, and vote for or against them as their judgement sees fit. In fact, the modern party system imposes overwhelming constraints.

The parties select candidates for elections in the first place, and their agents and activists work to ensure they are elected. In Parliament, each party maintains officials—members of Parliament aptly known as the Whips— who see to it that their members toe the approved line, with the ultimate sanction of withdrawing from recalcitrants all support at the next election. The governing party, with a host of junior appointments in its gift for the ambitious, can wave a carrot and a stick, and discipline is generally very strong.

As a result, a government is rarely defeated in the Commons. Should it be so, however, at any rate on a major issue such as the annual budget, the prime minister is obliged by constitutional convention to ask the monarch for a dissolution of Parliament, to be followed by a new general election. Elections, of course, have unpredictable results; and members of Parliament who indulge themselves in overthrowing governments may well find themselves seatless as a consequence. In 1979, when Prime Minister James Callaghan's shaky Labour Government was brought down by the shifting allegiance of various minor parties, he had the satisfaction of seeing them annihilated in the subsequent election— which also, unfortunately for him, drove the Labour Party itself into opposition. "This is the first time," James Callaghan told the House on the day of his downfall, "that the turkeys have voted for an early Christmas."

But a British prime minister need not wait for a defeat in the House of Commons before seeking a dissolution. He or she can "go to the country", in the British phrase, at any propitious moment in a Parliament's life—when opinion polls are favourable, say, or when the Opposition is in disarray. It is a prerogative much envied by leaders of other democracies, who must appear for re-election at a time that may not be of their choosing, and it ensures that British election campaigns are quick and relatively painless. There is rarely any sign of the paralysis that creeps over Washington, for example, when a presidential election approaches.

On the other hand, U.S. congressmen and senators enjoy a voting freedom, and hence a measure of personal authority, that British backbenchers have largely lost. But backbenchers— the term describes all members of Parliament who are neither government officeholders nor designated spokesmen for the Opposition—are by no means ciphers. Their most obvious opportunity to show their mettle is during question time, the hour set aside every day but Friday for members to air their grievances, demand an accounting from ministers, embarrass the government and otherwise gain themselves a little credit in their constituencies and the nation at large.

Question time sets the scene for confrontation. A well-researched and well-aimed question can leave a minister flailing helplessly. An adroit riposte, on the other hand, can greatly enhance the minister's standing, and since he has all the resources of the civil service staffing his department at his beck and call, the odds are strongly in his favour.

Less spectacularly and much more usefully, backbenchers can exercise their powers and intelligence on select committees, so-called because they are selected to reflect the distribution of parties in the House. There are standing committees on various areas of national interest: defence, for example, or public accounts. The most important role for backbench committeemen is during the progress of a bill through the Houses of Parliament until it becomes an act—and part of British law—or disappears without a trace. A bill begins with a first reading, a formal introduction that admits no debate. Next comes a second reading, when it is open to the full fury of parliamentary attack. Before the third and final reading, however, it passes through the committee stage, during which a select committee, free from the partisan clamour of the debating chamber, often amends it wisely and without too much party dogma. The third reading brings a final vote, after which the bill is passed on to the Lords for their (almost automatic) approval, then to Buckingham Palace for the (entirely automatic) royal assent that makes it law.

The House of Lords is composed of 26 bishops, together with the 800-odd hereditary peers—dukes, marquesses, earls, viscounts and barons—and more than 300 life peers—men and women appointed to the baronage for services to the nation, whose offspring will not inherit their titles. Among the life peers are some 20 senior judges, the active and retired Law Lords, for whom a peerage is as much a badge of office as their wigs and gowns. The 10 active Law Lords preside over the Common Law of England. The House of Lords is thus said to constitute the final court of

Framed between the royal emblems of a lion and a unicorn, the Chamber of the House of Lords provides a suitably sumptuous setting for lordly debate. Government supporters sit to the right of the throne, opponents to the left, and independents occupy central benches.

appeal in the English legal system—although it is the Law Lords alone, not the whole House, who hear a case.

Aside from this legal function, the House of Lords is of no great consequence in the modern constitution. From time to time there is talk of reforming it and providing Britain with some kind of elected second chamber, corresponding to the United States Senate. So far, such plans have always foundered, not before the reactionary obduracy of the Lords, but before the suspicious jealousy of the Commons, who rightly fear that their own power would be severely curtailed by a reformed House of Lords with a democratic legitimacy of its own.

From the nation at large there is little demand for the abolition of the House of Lords. Moreover, live radio and television coverage of the Lords' debates has greatly enhanced their reputation. Britons, listening to their legislators over their breakfast tables, are generally appalled at the noisy abuse that emanates from the House of Commons; and correspondingly impressed by the calm, courteous and frequently very well informed discussions in the more refined atmosphere of the Lords.

But of all Britain's ruling institutions it is the oldest and most anachronistic that, paradoxically, is thriving best. The monarchy is consistently high in public esteem, popular at every level of society. It has not always been so. For centuries, republican sentiment simmered in Britain, and only late in Queen Victoria's reign did it subside. Britain's Empire brought about the change: Victoria became a symbol of Britain's worldwide sway, and loyalty to her one facet of imperial pride.

Today, her descendant Queen Elizabeth, though no empress, symbolizes the fellowship of the Commonwealth—the association embracing most of Britain's ex-colonies—and she remains Head of State of a number of Commonwealth countries—Australia, for example. The title is of no practical consequence, but it means that in theory there is nothing to stop her from going to war with herself. And that is not the only logical contradiction. As heir of Henry VIII, for example, the Queen is head of the hierarchical and lavishly episcopal Church of England; as Queen of Scotland, however, she adroitly changes religion north of the border to become head of the sternly Presbyterian Church of Scotland.

The British people are not troubled by such details. To them, she is an immensely powerful living symbol, the personification of the state and a guarantee of its continuity. Today the monarchy is immaculate, untainted by the exercise of anything so coarse as power.

With the monarchy powerless and the Lords almost so, the authority of the House of Commons has never—on paper—been more absolute. In practice, however, the supremacy of the Commons has tended to diminish as other forces have grown in influence. Trades unions, industrial corporations and the City—home of the nation's great and immensely profitable financial institutions—are mighty centres of power that governments ignore at their peril. Since these interests are usually opposed and frequently in head-on confrontation, the role of the government has often been to juggle its way to some kind of temporary compromise.

The habit set in as long ago as the First World War, when British Cabinets strove for consensus between an unruly labour force and the profit-hungry businessmen who thrived in the

Margaret Thatcher seeks support from two of her constituents in the 1979 election that put the Conservatives into power and made her prime minister. In a British election campaign, even the party leaders are expected to do house-to-house canvassing.

booming wartime economy. By what amounted almost to a tacit amendment to Britain's already diffuse constitution, new elements—the leaders of British industry, and the representatives of labour—were allowed to share in the decision-making at the heart of the state. Today they exert their influence through contacts with the political parties and the administrators. (The American practice of lobbying individual politicians is much less important in Britain.) Employers' pressure groups can be sure of an attentive hearing when the Conservatives are in power; Labour governments are sympathetic to trade unionists' demands. Representatives from both sides of industry sit with civil servants on innumerable committees that advise the government on policy. With outsiders participating so closely, the clamour of parliamentary battle has become increasingly peripheral to the process of government.

Though British politicians have relinquished much of their initiative to interest groups, there is still one sense in which their powers are very great—some would say too great. For in Britain there is no law which clearly defines the prerogatives of the state and the rights of the individual. Its lack is occasionally felt. The effective power enjoyed by Britain's civil servants—and the vast numbers of administrators employed further down the pyramid of the state, in local government—is considerable. Moreover politicians and civil servants rarely allow the public to glimpse the reasoning behind their decisions. Their ingrained habits of secrecy can allow abuses to flourish that more open government would quickly eliminate. As the state develops bigger and bigger bureaucracies, extending

into more and more areas of life, aggrieved individuals find it increasingly difficult to obtain legal redress. Many in Britain believe that a bill embodying judicial reforms and written guarantees of basic liberties is overdue.

Defenders of the present arrangements point out that the tradition of political neutrality in the public service is very strong, even outside the ranks of career officials. In a sense this is true, despite rather than because of the system. The government, and in particular the prime minister, has immense powers of patronage, controlling appointments to the top jobs in every sphere of national life, from the judiciary to nationalized industries, from the BBC to the Church of England. Yet most such appointments are studiedly non-partisan; and though few prime ministers can resist the odd exception, British institutions are remarkably un-

burdened by direct political control. The BBC, for example, is free from state interference—even though the government, by means of TV licence revenue, provides its funds. The universities, also, are funded by central government yet are largely autonomous.

In fact, the libertarian social habits of the British are not protected by the constitution; the constitution is made workable by the people's habits. The governed have never much liked being pushed around by the governors; and the governors have rarely taken much pleasure in pushing them around. The British may love to dwell on Magna Carta and the antiquity of their institutions—but the surest guarantee of their rights and liberties is their modern-day resistance to being organized, patronized or bullied. It is not the sort of thing that is easily codified, but without it no legal code would function for long.

From the back of a glass-roofed Rolls-Royce, the Queen greets the crowds who have lined the streets to watch her pass on the way to an engagement.

THE MONARCHY ON DISPLAY

An anomalous institution in a democratic age, the British monarchy still casts a potent spell over subjects and foreigners alike. Aloofness is essential to its magic: the grandeur of state occasions and the invisible barriers of protocol lend a mystique which Queen Elizabeth II would never shatter by riding a bicycle or granting an interview with a journalist. Her devotion to duty and exemplary family life strengthen the respect in which her people hold her.

The Queen is Britain's politically neutral Head of State, and as such she plays a valuable diplomatic role, travelling extensively abroad and receiving high-ranking foreign visitors to Britain. Among her own people, she is constantly in demand to confer honours, inspect soldiers, open new institutions and grace charity events with her presence. She shares these duties with her children, her husband, her sister, mother, aunt and cousins. They undertake some 2,000 engagements a year among them, and receive a handsome income out of public funds for their services. These payments, together with the upkeep of the royal palaces, the royal yacht and the royal train, cost the British taxpayer around £20 million a year. Few would deny, however, that the "family firm", as the late King George VI referred to his hard-working relations, gives good value.

Three times a year, the Queen escapes the treadmill of public events and retires to the countryside to relax with her family, ride her horses and walk her dogs. Her house parties are on a scale that very few of her subjects could emulate—but her taste for simple, rustic pursuits is one that most of them share. Though set apart from her people, she epitomizes them all, and thus draws them together as no other national institution can.

QUEEN
VICTORIA
1819–1901
m
Prince Albert
of Saxe-Coburg
and Gotha
1819–1861

Victoria
Princess Royal
1840–1901

THE ROYAL FAMILY TREE

Both the Queen and her husband
Prince Philip trace their descent from
Queen Victoria, the great-great-
grandmother of the reigning monarch.
The lines of descent, respectively from
Victoria's eldest son King Edward VII
and from Princess Alice, the second
of her five daughters, are traced here
down to the present generation.
Numerals beneath some living
members of the family show the
present order of succession. Charles,
Prince of Wales, is the heir apparent,
as the monarch's eldest son; his
children, William and Henry, are
next in line to the throne. The only
daughter, Princess Anne, ranks sixth,
behind her younger brothers Andrew
and Edward, because the rule of
succession ordains that male heirs
take precedence over their female
counterparts.

KING
EDWARD VIII
1894–1972
m
Wallis Simpson
1896–1986

KING
GEORGE VI
1895–1952
m
Lady Elizabeth
Bowes-Lyon
(Queen Elizabeth
the Queen Mother)
1900–

QUEEN
ELIZABETH II
1926–
m
Philip
Duke of Edinburgh
1921–

Princess
Margaret
1930–
9
m
Antony
Earl of Snowdon
1930–

(Divorced 1978)

David
Viscount Linley
1961–
10

Lady Sarah
Armstrong-Jones
1964–
11

Charles
Prince of Wales
1948–
1
m
Lady Diana
Spencer
1961–

Princess Anne
1950–
6
m
Captain
Mark Phillips
1948–

Prince Andrew
Duke of York
1960–
4
m
Sarah Ferguson
1959–

Prince Edward
1964–
5

Peter Phillips
1977–
7

Zara Phillips
1981–
8

Prince William
of Wales
1982–
2

Prince Henry
1984–
9

KING EDWARD VII 1841–1910	m Princess Alexandra of Denmark 1844–1925	Princess Alice 1843–1878 m Grand Duke Louis of Hesse 1837–1892	Alfred Duke of Edinburgh 1844–1900	Princess Helena 1846–1923	Princess Louise 1848–1939	Arthur Duke of Connaught 1850–1942	Leopold Duke of Albany 1853–1884	Princess Beatrice 1857–1944

Victoria 1863–1950   m   Louis, Marquess of Milford Haven 1854–1921   Alix of Hesse 1872–1918   m   Nicholas II Tsar of Russia 1868–1918

Princess Alice 1885–1969   m   Prince Andrew of Greece 1882–1944   George, Marquess of Milford Haven 1892–1938   Louis Earl Mountbatten of Burma 1900–1979

Philip Duke of Edinburgh 1921–

Albert Victor Duke of Clarence 1864–1892	KING GEORGE V 1865–1936 m	Princess Mary of Teck 1867–1953	Louise Princess Royal 1867–1931	Princess Victoria 1868–1935	Princess Maud 1869–1938

Mary Princess Royal 1897–1965 m Henry Earl of Harewood 1882–1947	Henry Duke of Gloucester 1900–1974 m Lady Alice Montagu Douglas Scott 1901–	George Duke of Kent 1902–1942 m Princess Marina of Greece 1906–1968	Prince John 1905–1919

Prince William 1941–1972   Richard Duke of Gloucester 1944– **12**   m   Birgitte van Deurs 1946–

Alexander Earl of Ulster 1974– **13**	Lady Davina Windsor 1977– **14**	Lady Rose Windsor 1980– **15**

Edward Duke of Kent 1935– **16**   m   Katharine Worsley 1933–   Princess Alexandra 1936–   m   Honourable Angus Ogilvy 1928–   Prince Michael 1942–   m   Baroness Marie-Christine von Reibnitz 1945–

George Earl of St Andrews 1962– **17**	Lady Helen Windsor 1964– **19**	Lord Nicholas Windsor 1970– **18**	James Ogilvy 1964–	Marina Ogilvy 1966–	Lord Frederick Windsor 1979– **20** Lady Gabriella Windsor 1981– **21**

Surrounded by other members of the Royal Family and their guests, the Queen and her consort wave to spectators from the balcony of Buckingham Palace at the end of the Trooping the Colour ceremony. This military pageant marks the Queen's "official" birthday each June—celebrated then when there is a good chance of fine weather, although her real birthday is in April. In full view, from left to right, are the Duke of Kent, Princess Alexandra, Lord Nicholas Windsor, Princess Anne, the Duke of Edinburgh, the Queen, Peter Phillips, Prince Charles, Lord Frederick Windsor, Princess Diana, Queen Elizabeth the Queen Mother and Lady Rose Windsor.

At the annual royal garden party in the grounds of Holyroodhouse in Edinburgh, where the Queen spends a week each summer, guests awaiting the Queen form a ring *(left)* at a respectful distance from the spot where she will stand. Only a privileged few are formally presented to her *(inset)*.

The Queen and Prince Philip take part in a parade at Windsor Castle during the annual ceremony of the Order of the Garter. Admission to this company of knights, founded in 1348, is in the gift of the Queen. Most other honours, though awarded in her name, are dispensed by the prime minister.

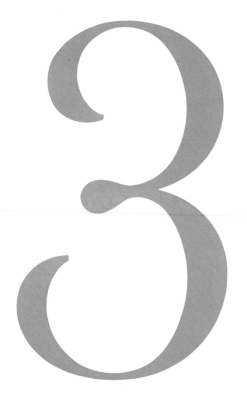

Waiting for her sister to finish her ballet lesson, a tired child snuggles up to her nanny. The young woman wears the uniform of Norland College, the cream of nursery training establishments, whose graduates are much in demand to care for the children of Britain's aristocracy.

A STRATIFIED SOCIETY

One of the funniest books to reach Britain's bestseller charts in 1982 was *The Official Sloane Ranger Handbook*. It describes with devastating precision the identifying marks and the lifestyle of a minute but very visible subsection of the British population—those who are located near the apex of society, whose moderate wealth derives from the achievements of their 19th-century forebears in business, but whose values come from the older, rural world of the aristocracy. "Sloane Rangerhood is a state of mind that's eternal," says the introduction; "you might believe it's all different now, that nobody's like that anymore. You'd be wrong."

The Sloane Ranger, named after Chelsea's Sloane Square—the centre of her world—can be identified in town by her navy-blue pleated skirt, her healthy pink cheeks, her bicycle and her pearls; in the country, her uniform includes green wellingtons and a green quilted jacket. The youthful Sloane Ranger works as a secretary in London's art world or in publishing, or cooks lunches for the directors' dining room of an old-established London firm. Her male counterpart is established in the City or the law, or perhaps the army. They both love horses and dogs and anything to do with the land, and spend nearly every weekend in the country.

In the Sloane subculture, rules of dress and deportment matter deeply. "Sloane men go in for fraud and adultery in later life with far fewer qualms than into a frilled nylon evening shirt." Possessions are treasured not for their expense—"no mink, please, we're *old* money"—but for their age and for the traditions they embody; "The whole Sloane ethos is based on handing things down."

This elaborate code keeps non-Sloanes at bay, and it is reinforced by the exclusiveness of Sloane social life. A Sloane girl meets eligible men not at work but at drinks and dinner parties, and always through a mutual acquaintance. "This means you can make automatic assumptions about the background, behaviour, and *character* of any man you meet. No one entirely unsuitable would be there in the first place. It's one of the most subtle vetting systems in the world."

The Sloane Ranger is a very British phenomenon, and so is the delight the wider public took in reading about her. The German sociologist Ralf Dahrendorf, who worked in London from 1974 to 1984, found the passion for layering and labelling society one of the most notable and curious features of the British. Fine distinctions, he wrote, "are given meaning and turned into worlds of difference... Every estate resulting from this process has its own symbols, rules and above all boundaries."

Speech offers the British some of their best opportunities for sorting out social position. "An Englishman's way of speaking absolutely classifies him," wrote George Bernard Shaw in 1912. Accents are the first clue. Regional accents—with the single exception of the Edinburgh accent, which is perfectly genteel—are found only at the lower levels of society, and those who talk in the plums-in-the-mouth tones of society's upper reaches can pick out an intruder from the slip of a single vowel.

Choice of words can be as informative as accents to those attuned to the signals. People who call their midday meal "lunch" and people who call it "dinner" inhabit different spheres, and a gulf separates those who say "horse-riding" and those who take the horse for granted and simply say "riding". Names, too, convey a message. Caroline is Sloane Ranger, Carol suggests distinctly lower origins. The satirical magazine *Private Eye* provokes a chuckle by referring to the Queen and the Duke of Edinburgh as Brenda and Keith, names redolent of suburbia.

The society that makes these endless fine distinctions is also very aware of two steep gradations. The first falls between Britain's working class and its middle class—roughly, that is, between the manual and the non-manual workers. And at the top of society, the middle class shades into something that is perceptibly different—an upper class whose tone is set by the aristocracy and the country gentry.

In numerous surveys over the past few decades, cross-sections of the British population have been asked to assign themselves to a class, and without prompting at least 90 per cent have placed themselves in one of the three

3

categories—upper, middle or working—or a subdivision of them, such as lower-middle. In one such survey, conducted in 1983, only 6 per cent of those questioned mentioned substantially different categories, such as "poor" or "ordinary", or failed altogether to grasp the idea of class.

The 1983 survey showed that a little under half the population thinks of itself as working class, a little over half as middle class. Virtually nobody claimed to be upper class. On the face of it, this is evidence of recent change in British society, because surveys in the 1940s, 50s and 60s regularly reported that about 2 per cent called itself upper class. But the recent survey must be interpreted with caution. "Upper class" is no longer a term in common use; to avoid charges of snobbery, the British have found all sorts of euphemisms ("Sloane Ranger" is just one) to express essentially the same idea. The social historian Arthur Marwick considers the upper class still make up about 2 per cent of the population.

Notwithstanding such complications, the British response to questions about class is far more clear-cut than that of other nations. A large majority of Americans consider themselves middle class, if anything; to many, the questions have no meaning. In other European countries the issue is confused by the existence or recent disappearance of a large peasant population, and the categories people use overlap far more than in Britain.

To sociologists, a person's class is determined by his job and the pay he receives. Sociologists distinguish class from what they call "status"—that is, a person's lifestyle and his consequent position in the social hierarchy. But ordinary British people's understanding of the word "class" is a fusion of the sociologists' two concepts. In everyday English, class is an amalgam of how a person earns his money and what he does with it. His job is the single most

74

crucial indication of his class, but the subtle distinctions of lifestyle and manners must also be weighed in the balance, and many go against the evidence of the job.

Because money limits what lifestyles are available to an individual, it determines his position in society in the long term. But in the short term, a person can conform to the mores of a class without having the appropriate job or income. An impoverished old lady living out her days in a Bournemouth hotel might legitimately claim to be upper class because of her connections and her familiarity with aristocratic conventions. Equally, a self-made millionaire from London's working-class heartland, the East End, might drive around in a Rolls Royce but continue to consider himself a member of the class into which he was born.

These occasional divergences between class and income help to illuminate Britain's peculiarities. Every country has inequalities of wealth and income, and resulting gradations of status, but elsewhere the inequalities are not translated so relentlessly into nuances of lifestyle, which in Britain take on an importance of their own.

If any one group of people is responsible for the peculiar pervasiveness of class in Britain, it is the aristocracy. The aristocrats are numbered only in thousands and their political power as a class today is negligible. The rest of society could ignore them if it chose. But the aristocrats' strength is that they have persuaded those beneath them to see things their way. And their picture of Britain is a pre-industrial, rural one, in which society is graded into many ranks—grouped into upper, middling and lower—and the hereditary land-owners occupy the uppermost layers. In other words, the aristocrats place themselves at the apex, because even today they are among Britain's biggest landowners. The Duke of Westminster owns 120 hectares of central London and a substantial part of Cheshire; the Marquess of Salisbury has 2,800 hectares surrounding his family seat in Hertfordshire and not much less at his other residence, in Dorset; the Earl of Cawdor owns 22,500 hectares of Scottish farms and moorland.

Because Britain has escaped great political upheavals in the past few hundred years, the aristocracy is still firmly entrenched in the constitution. While titles in other European countries have become meaningless, British peers retain their seats in the House of Lords. This is part of the explanation for the aristocracy's continued influence. But its real secret is and always has been its openness. It has never despised *nouveaux riches*: it embraces them, provided they are prepared to change their ways. And when ordinary people can aspire to the aristocracy, their desire to abolish it becomes curiously muted.

Even in past centuries, British aristocrats married freely with the daughters of the country gentry and—rather less freely—with the daughters of rich merchants. Moreover, a commoner who acquired a sizeable estate could be sure, sooner or later, of being ennobled. Conversely, younger sons of aristocrats have never succeeded to their father's title, nor have they received a share in the family land; they were expected to make their own way in the world.

The French political philosopher Alexis de Tocqueville, who travelled around England in 1833, saw clearly the consequences of such customs. He had arrived in England expecting to find the same revolutionary egalitarian fervour that had erupted in France 40 years earlier. Instead, de Tocqueville noted, "in general one can say that the aristocracy is founded on wealth, a thing which may be *acquired*, and not on birth which cannot... The English aristocracy can therefore never arouse those violent hatreds felt by the middle and lower classes against the nobility in France where the nobility is an exclusive caste."

Although the England that de Tocqueville observed seemed so stable compared with France, the industrial revolution that had begun in the previous century was already wreaking changes in British society. Many new fortunes were being made from the cotton mills and steel foundries, and from the banks that financed growth and trade. Yet the emergence of a wealthy entrepreneurial group did not affect the aristocrats' standing. The new money was seduced by the ways of the old. Successful financiers and industrialists retired from their labours, bought country estates and integrated themselves into country life; peerages often followed. The upper class was expanding, it was becoming more diverse in its origins, but its values remained the same as ever.

The Sloane Rangers, today's descendants of the 19th-century newcomers, are hard to distinguish from the aristocracy. And the process of confusing worldly success with birth and breeding still continues—in both directions. Outstanding careers in the civil service or industry, on the stage or in Parliament, are rewarded by a knighthood or a peerage. Conversely, an aristocrat who desires a career in business or finance will have no trouble accumulating

Young socialites relax at the annual Rose Ball, held in London in mid-May to raise money for charity. For debutantes—girls being launched by their parents into fashionable adult society—the occasion is a high point in a hectic, four-month social season.

TOP HATS AT THE TURF

Royal Ascot, held over four afternoons towards the end of June, is England's most glamorous horse-racing event. Enthusiasts of the turf converge on the 4-kilometre course near the village of Ascot in Berkshire, not only to watch top-class horses competing for prestigious prizes but also to catch a glimpse of royalty at close quarters.

Five horse-drawn landaus bring the Queen with her family and friends to the racetrack every day from nearby Windsor Castle; just before the start of the afternoon's racing, the royal entourage drives in stately procession up the course.

The smartest place from which to watch the race is the Royal Enclosure, where the Queen herself sits. Anyone aspiring to a place there must pay a substantial fee and be sponsored by someone who has attended regularly. For women, hats are obligatory; for men, required wear is formal morning dress, including top hat and tailcoat. In their finery, the lucky few picnic and drink champagne before settling down to watch the day's events.

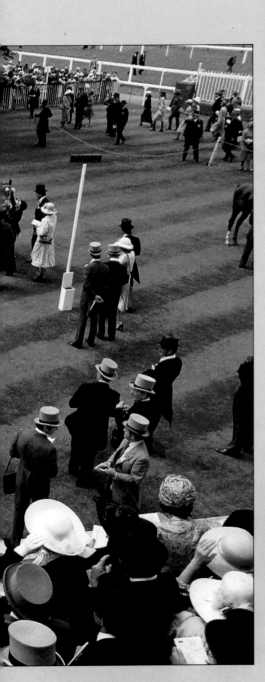

While some chatter, the more single-minded spectators follow the action.

After a race, the winning horses are led into the Unsaddling Enclosure to be greeted by owners and trainers. The Queen or another member of the Royal Family will present the trophies.

Elaborately attired in pastel shades, a woman racegoer chats to one of the officials manning the gate of the Enclosure. Ascot is the scene for much sartorial competition, and occasionally hats reach ludicrous proportions.

3

directorships of companies or establishing himself in the City.

Nowadays, land ownership is no longer a prerequisite for membership of Britain's fuzzy-edged upper class. The potent attraction of land remains evident, however, in the upper-class lifestyle. The sports of the aristocracy are hunting, game shooting and fishing for trout or salmon; all require one's own expanses or access to someone else's. Horse races are among the great social events of the year. And recognizably upper-class clothes are country clothes—tweed suits, hand-made boots—preferably with a patina of age and wear, to indicate that their owner has nothing to prove.

Those who remain landowners on a large scale see the family estates as the central part of their heritage. They generally maintain close ties with, and a strong sense of responsibility towards, the local community, and an even stronger awareness of the future generations of their families for whom they hold the property in trust. Today, exercising that trust is a delicate business. Often the most problematical part of their inheritance is the gracious house built by some distant ancestor for a lifestyle which even the rich cannot contemplate nowadays. To keep the roof in repair, thousands of owners of great houses all over Britain now open their doors to paying sightseers. They do not enjoy the loss of their privacy but the alternative—selling the house—is still more painful.

Richard Bridgeman, Seventh Earl of Bradford, is tackling the problems of the 20th-century landed aristocrat more radically than most. He came into his title and property in 1981, at the age of 34. Along with Weston Park, the 17th-century family seat in Shrop-shire with its extensive park and 4,800 hectares of farmland, he inherited an alarming tax bill and the prospect of vast upkeep costs for years to come.

His grandfather, to make life agreeable in Weston Park, employed 34 domestic servants and 35 gardeners. His father lived there in less style, but even so the house was a colossal drain on the family finances. The seventh earl decided that he had to move out. He and his family live in a converted farmhouse on the estate, "very comfortably, happily and affordably". The house, with its old-master paintings, its tapestries and antique furniture, is open to the public. Outbuildings house an aquarium and a "museum of country bygones". Lord Bradford has been careful not to let any garish commercialism intrude on either the architecture or the wooded setting. Other stately home owners have converted their grounds into safari parks or funfairs, and in Lord Bradford's opinion, "a lot spoiled their own heritage".

In his twenties, he went into the catering business, founding and running a succession of fashionable restaurants in London and Brighton. Now, drawing upon his catering experience, he organizes conferences and lavish dinners at Weston Park, often doing the cooking himself. He works hard, not to keep himself in great luxury but to make the house self-supporting and maintain the status quo. What matters to him is that the next generation should receive its inheritance intact.

The concept of the gentleman, according to philosopher Bertrand Russell, was invented by the aristocracy to keep the middle classes in order. The aristocracy evidently hit upon a powerful formula because in 1982 Ralf Dahrendorf could write, "England's middle class is not harassed and ambitious, but happy and acquiescent. It is not a ruling middle class nor one that is driven by a ceaseless hunger for more."

In the 19th century, when it emerged as a distinct group, Britain's middle class was ambitious and by no means acquiescent. Proud of creating and running the industry that was making Britain rich, it extolled the benefits of capital and the virtues of competition,

Amid flowers arranged by some of the flock, parishioners join their vicar in celebrating Sunday matins in a Suffolk church. In the early 1950s, nearly 10 per cent of the population attended church regularly, but by the early 1980s the figure was only 3 per cent.

Their pints of beer temporarily set aside, lunchtime drinkers concentrate on a game of dominoes in a pub in the seaport of Hull. Public houses are judged largely by the quality of their beer, but many offer such additional attractions as darts or snooker.

self-help and thrift. Middle classes in other countries caught on to the same ideas and still hold fast to them today; the ideal is to do better all the time.

But in Britain, before the end of the 19th century, an influential section of the new middle class came under the spell of the aristocracy. Even those who did not rise to enter the ranks of the upper class came to accept some of its values, as they still do today. The middle classes look back to the pre-industrial rural world as the real Britain and see the industry their ancestors generated as something of an aberration. They view excessive materialism as vulgar. They share the aristocrats' sense of social responsibility, though they are more likely to express it by working for charities and paying their taxes without too many grumbles than by serving their immediate community. Their lifestyle has acquired many other echoes of the aristocrat's. A country estate is out of reach, but a detached or semi-detached suburban villa with a garden is an attainable ideal. They may not be invited to shooting parties on Scottish moors, but they can enjoy the wide vistas of the local golf course. They are excluded from the glamorous social round, but they entertain on a modest scale in their homes and cherish their leisure. Informality and faded comfort are the effects they strive for in their homes and their clothes.

Of course, not every middle-class family in Britain wishes, even subconsciously, to emulate the aristocracy. In his book about the middle classes, Ian Bradley identifies four categories of middle-classness: "The professional upper middle classes have always prided themselves on their culture, their liberal values and their tolerance. The up-and-coming middle classes have always made virtues of ambition and competition. The lower middle classes have always been preoccupied with propriety and decency, with doing the right thing, and keep their distance from the working classes. The anti-establishment rebels have always attacked the rest of the middle classes for their snobbery, their materialism, their puritanism and their philistinism."

The differences run deep enough to prevent the British middle classes from speaking with one voice. They read different national newspapers and, though a majority of them vote Conservative, they are by no means uniformly enthusiastic about the party. The professional group are the most consistent Conservative voters, while the anti-establishment group are likely to vote anything but Conservative. Within the up-and-coming group, a very sizeable minority vote Labour.

In spite of their differences, the subsections of the middle class do share some common traits. More than three quarters of them own their houses. They are generally prepared to move house for the sake of a new job or promotion, and are not at all likely to live in the same place throughout their lives. The factor that will make them hesitate before moving is the disruption to their children's schooling, because they are ambitious for their children even if not always for themselves. They retain their 19th-century habits of thrift, saving more money than the working classes.

They value privacy and independence. Middle-class families are chary of becoming too intimate with neighbours, and they generally holiday as an independent unit. On the other hand, the middle classes participate enthusiastically in any organization that links people with a common interest. They belong to political parties in much larger numbers than the working class. They throng to parent-teacher organizations, pressure groups for the preservation of Victorian architecture or patches of countryside, mutual support groups for new mothers or single-parent families. Relatively few Britons are active church members but the middle classes participate more than most. They see themselves, and

3

with much justice, as the guardians of Britain's social fabric.

To foreigners, the most surprising fact about the British working class is that it exists at all. "On the Continent," writes Ralf Dahrendorf, "the expression 'working class' is most likely to be used by intellectual agitators. . . Everybody likes to call himself a 'worker', or at any rate to indicate that he works, and works hard, for a living; but the notion of a working class with its own boundaries, rules and symbols seems strange to most Frenchmen or Germans, or for that matter Americans."

One reason why the British have developed a distinct working-class culture is simply that they have had more time to do so than other nations. Until the end of the 18th century, society's "lower orders" lacked a sense of common identity; their most important relations were not with each other but with people further up the social hierarchy. The force that changed these relations was industrialization. The manufacturing revolution which began in the late 18th century had within a few decades spawned dozens of new cities and towns to house factory workers. The new industrial proletariat crammed into the squalid streets lost contact with other ranks of society. By the 1820s, they had acquired a sense of themselves as a separate class whose interests were more often than not opposed to those of their employers. To this day, the working class holds fast to its separate identity.

Germany and the United States were not far behind Britain in the race to industrialize, and new urban communities grew up there as well. But in the United States any sense of working-class solidarity has been counteracted by the emphasis on competition and individual ambition, and in Germany the period of reconstruction after World War II helped to iron out class differences. So Britain—peculiar anyway in retaining some of the subtle gradations of the pre-industrial world—is doubly peculiar in that it superimposes on those gradations a strongly felt industrial class system.

Solidarity is the most distinctive feature of the working-class culture. It expresses itself first in the strength of family and neighbourhood ties. Working-class children usually live with their parents until they marry and sometimes even afterwards. When they do move away, it is often only a few streets' distance, and they maintain almost daily contact. Neighbours take endless interest in each other's doings, help each other out with gifts and loans, and between them care for the community's old and sick.

To research his 1979 study, *A Tale of Five Cities*, the journalist John Ardagh stayed in provincial cities of five European countries; Newcastle-upon-Tyne, his choice for England, is an overwhelmingly working-class city and it struck Ardagh forcibly with its "real ambience of caring and kindness". Here, he writes, "concern is manifest at every level—in the services run so enthusiastically by the city council's staff, in the numerous volunteer organizations, and in streets and suburbs where people group spontaneously to help each other. This social action is far more marked than in my other cities."

The caring spirit found in a healthy working-class community is far from indestructible. In the 1960s, many badly housed working-class communities were moved to high-rise flats where the old habits of neighbourly contact and street-corner gossip were much harder to maintain. Often such developments degenerated into slums. A sudden influx of immigrants is another strain to which many working-class districts have been subjected in the past few decades. For a class which sets much store by its shared history and background, accepting newcomers with very different lifestyles has not been easy.

But the working-class community spirit is robust enough to withstand mere relocation and, though it sprang up in conditions of great poverty, it survives even in affluence. John Ardagh found that the Newcastle families moved by the local authorities from the decaying city centre to comfortable new suburbs quickly re-created their civic spirit. He discovered neighbourhood social clubs of all kinds, and groups of families who had pooled their resources to buy a lawnmower and who shared it in perfect harmony.

Working-class pleasures are on the whole gregarious. There are plenty of exceptions—the solitary joys of pigeon breeding or allotment gardening, for instance—but they are for minorities. Most people drink not at home but in the pub or, in northern cities such as Newcastle, a working men's club. Almost two million people regularly crowd the grandstands to watch football matches on Saturday afternoons. The typical working-class holiday in the first half of the century was a day trip to the seaside with a coachload of neighbours or workmates. Now the destination is as likely to be Majorca as Blackpool, but the aeroplane will be filled with friends and acquaintances whose company will make the foreign destination a home from home.

The working-class ethos of togetherness can sometimes stunt individual enterprise. Getting on in the world may mean saying goodbye to one's mates, and for some the sacrifice outweighs the reward. But what the working class lacks in individual aspiration it has made up for in group endeavour. Many institutions flourishing today bear witness to the determination of successive working-class generations to better their lot by group action.

Not all these institutions have turned out quite as their founders imagined. "Co-operative" societies mushroomed in the 19th century as a revolutionary, if non-violent, attempt to opt out of capitalism. Pockets of working-class people all over the country set up shops in which everyone who bought the goods had a stake. The idea was that the profits which came back to the purchasers would generate further growth, and gradually the autonomous co-operative groups would extend until they meshed with one another. But the means overtook the ends, and today the only witnesses to the brave adventure are Co-op supermarkets and other services, scattered up and down the land, which are owned and controlled by the 10 million co-operative members.

Building societies were another working-class invention, one that was designed to counter the difficulty of finding rented accommodation in the growing industrial cities. In the early days, each member of a building society was someone who wanted accommodation, and who contributed an amount of money to the society every week; when enough had been collected it was used to buy land and build houses. By the early 19th century, building societies had begun to accept funds from people who did not want to buy a house but who were looking for somewhere to invest their money. To-

Outside the pigeon shed in his back garden, a Yorkshire miner feeds pedigree birds he has reared. Long-distance pigeon-racing is a popular sport in working-class districts of the north of England.

day, building societies play a prominent part in national life—six million house-buyers are paying off loans from building societies and 25 million people have building-society savings accounts—but they have lost their exclusively working-class associations.

Two working-class institutions which today retain the spirit of their founders are the Labour Party and the trade union movement. They remain the focus of much working-class feeling. Throughout the whole post-war period, about 80 per cent of male manual workers have belonged to a trade union and 75 per cent of the working class have voted Labour.

Tom Milan, a retired postman who lives in the Walthamstow district of east London, sees himself as atypical of the working classes in some respects: he does not go to football matches, he does not drink, and his hobbies—reading and painting—are typical middle-class pursuits. But he has voted Labour and been a union man all his life; he finds it a source of pride that working men created the trade unions.

He sees the unions' role as protecting the poor against the privileged and dislikes "modern-type union leaders with high salaries like rich men" who seem to him to betray the union ideals. The middle classes "get a tremendous amount of money without ever doing a day's work" and the working classes, he feels, are further than ever from attaining their degree of privilege. Yet some people, he fears, may be in danger of forgetting it. "A lot are blindfolded by the fact that they've got their own house and car. They're being hoaxed by the government the whole time."

Tom Milan is aware that his own chances were blighted unnecessarily. An intelligent man, he barely learnt to

3

read and write at school in the 1930s because classes had 50 pupils and the teachers did not care. One told his pupils, "It's not worth trying to teach you anything, you'll just be fodder for the next war." Ever after, Tom Milan felt handicapped by his education, particularly his inability to spell. Lacking confidence, he never accepted promotion. "It terrified me; in my heart, I knew something would let me down."

His children have taken advantage of opportunities that were denied him. All three went to university or college. His son emigrated to Australia, where he runs a radio station. One of his daughters is an actress, the other a commercial artist. Their successes gratify Tom Milan, but they do not efface his regret at not having bettered himself. What he minds most is not having saved enough to buy a house. When he dies, he will have nothing to leave his wife and family—and that, to him, spells failure.

In the 50 years since Tom Milan's sorry experience of school, much has changed for the better in British education. Yet discrepancies remain, making education the most socially divisive aspect of British society. Children of different classes are segregated into different sorts of school—the independent, fee-charging schools for a minority and the free, state-run system for the vast majority. Because it is so bound up with class, education is a sensitive political issue in Britain. Changes are instigated or opposed as much in the interest of social engineering as to meet the needs of individual children or their future employers.

In the state-run sector, a child attends a primary school until the age of 11, then a secondary school until at least 16. Up to the 1970s, there were two major categories of secondary school—grammar schools and secondary moderns. Secondary moderns gave a limited education to the majority of children. Grammar schools were designed for the academic 25 per cent of children who worked towards the examinations which would provide a passport to higher education. While the vast majority of state schools have always been financed and run by local authorities, there existed a special category of grammar schools, with exceptionally high standards, which were subsidized by a grant from central government. These were known as direct-grant schools.

An examination taken at the age of 11 determined each child's destiny. In practice, the secondary schools' intake replicated the divisions of the social structure. Working-class children predominated in the secondary moderns. Middle-class children, benefiting from encouragement and help at home, passed the crucial examination and went on to make up two thirds of the grammar school population. For upper-middle-class parents, direct-grant schools were very acceptable alternatives to private education.

The state system was set up in this form in 1944, but already by the 1950s it was attracting much criticism. Many felt that it was iniquitous and wasteful of resources to classify children into sheep and goats at the tender age of 11. A few local authorities merged their streams of secondary education into "comprehensive" schools which catered for all levels of ability. In 1964, the Labour government announced its commitment to comprehensive education and the pace of change accelerated. By 1971, 38 per cent of secondary pupils in the state system attended comprehensive schools. Thirteen years later, that proportion had risen to 84 per cent and all the direct-grant schools had become private or disappeared.

Each transition was painful. Thousands of excellent schools were abolished. The loss of the direct-grant schools, a fast route to the top for many bright, poor children in the past, was especially regretted. Discipline was often hard to maintain in the big new comprehensives. Many people feared that the zeal for equality would force down academic standards at the top. Most, however, now agree that the change had to come, and that the comprehensives should not be judged on their turbulent early years. They need time to settle and establish their own traditions.

But the picture that is emerging is of great diversity. Each comprehensive has its own specialities and weaknesses. Some are almost as academically competitive as the old grammar schools, while others maintain that the individual child's opportunities for self-expression must be paramount.

If the advent of the comprehensives has at least partially bridged one class gap in British education, it has only reinforced another—that between the state system and the private schools which educate 6 per cent of British children. The proportion of children in private education had been declining from a level of over 9 per cent in 1951, but once grammar schools started disappearing it abruptly stabilized.

Independent schools for girls follow roughly the state pattern: girls attend their first school from age five to 11, and their second school takes them up to school-leaving age. A boy's education has an extra division: he first

FUN BESIDE THE SEASIDE

The seaside holiday became Britain's favourite summer leisure institution by a process of democratization. It was the upper class of the 18th century that first became enamoured of sea bathing and made towns such as Brighton and Southend fashionable. The middle classes soon followed in their footsteps. But by the mid-19th century, railways connected the burgeoning manufacturing cities with the coast, and factory workers began to discover the delights of a trip to the seaside. Today, many Britons holiday abroad too, but the 10 most popular British coastal resorts each still receive more than a million visitors a year.

The pleasures awaiting the holidaymakers are hallowed by tradition. If the seafront is graced with one of Britain's many ornate Victorian piers, they can wander along to the pavilion at the far end to enjoy a drink over the waves. A brass band may be playing at a nearby bandstand, in which case they can drowse to its strains in a deckchair. Funfairs, bingo and stalls selling vinegar-soaked whelks provide more entertainment, but the sea itself is the main attraction.

The British climate is rarely ideal for sea bathing, but holidaymakers do not let that interfere with their fun. Defying inclement weather, they picnic on the sand in coats and scarves, then bravely expose pale, goose-pimpled flesh to the numbing water. The discomfort suffered in the name of pleasure baffles outsiders, but for the British it is just part of the ritual of being beside the sea.

At Llandudno, a large resort on the north Wales coast, holidaymakers stroll along an ornately decorated pier. Originally landing stages for boats, piers developed in the 19th century into extensions of the seafront promenade, bulging with kiosks offering snacks and entertainments.

Children line up their donkeys for a race across the sands at Skegness in Lincolnshire—a favourite resort for workers in Britain's industrial Midlands. Behind the young jockeys the disused remnants of a storm-damaged pier rise out of the sea.

A gaily striped windbreak shelters a circle of friends on the beach at Blackpool, on the north-west coast. Britain's most popular seaside resort, it draws some eight million people a year—half in September and October, when the illuminations along the 11-kilometre promenade are turned on.

After a cursory paddle, holiday companions gingerly return to dry land up the shingle beach at Brighton, best-known of England's south coast resorts. Behind them, the Palace Pier stretches 541 metres out to sea.

3

attends a junior school, then a "prep" school from age eight to 13, and finally a "public" school from 13 to 18.

Some of the best-known public schools are very old indeed. Winchester was founded by Bishop William of Wykeham in 1382, Eton by King Henry VI in 1440. (At the time of their founding they provided free places for ordinary local people, hence the name "public" school.) But the distinctive ethos of public schools traces back to the 19th century, when Britain's Empire was expanding and a confident, high-minded élite was needed to man its outposts. Dozens of new public schools appeared and the old ones were recast as nurseries for empire-builders. The novelist Anthony Powell, who attended Eton just after World War I, recalls that, "it was assumed, or so it seemed to me, that every boy would at one time or another be in some such position as Viceroy of India and must be brought up with this end in view."

The end was not to be achieved solely, or even chiefly, through study. Some public schools—Winchester is one—have always prided themselves on the highest academic standards. But an emphasis on character-building was the public schools' hallmark.

The school chapel was a focal point and team games mattered as much as lessons. So that they would acquire habits of leadership, older boys were charged with keeping discipline, and allowed to enforce it with floggings. Most public schools were and still are boarding schools, so the special atmosphere created in an all-male society with its own private rules and rites was heightened by the boys' isolation from the world for nine months of the year.

Nowadays, public schools are not quite such esoteric places. They allow more visits home during terms and many have gone co-educational; floggings by boys have been abolished. But they still confer a special social status on their pupils. Virtually all upper-class parents send their children to public schools, as do a fair proportion of professional upper-middle-class parents. Any child from a less exalted background sent to a public school has a good chance of picking up upper-class habits of mind and emerging as a fully integrated member of the élite.

"The old school tie" can mean friends and influence in high places for the rest of one's life. The more prestigious the school, the more doors it opens. At the apex, Eton constitutes "not only an educational establishment but a political training ground, a charm school and a unique national network", as Anthony Sampson puts it in his *Anatomy of Britain*. The power of that formula can be seen in the concentration of men from a few schools occupying Britain's top jobs. In 1982, Eton and Winchester men between them occupied the chairmanships of all five of the nation's major banks, the two top posts at the state-funded broadcasting service, the BBC, the editorship of the most prestigious daily newspaper, *The Times*, and the top posts in the home and foreign civil service. In the 1979–83 Parliament, 50 of the 635 members of Parliament were Old Etonians.

But no matter how much ambitious parents value connections and moral fibre, the priority for most of them nowadays is a rigorous academic education. The public schools have recognized this and since the 1970s have been putting increasing emphasis on getting their pupils through examinations. Today they set tough entrance requirements and justify themselves to parents by the promise of first-rate teaching leading to first-rate careers.

In a few areas of employment, notably the City, connections and social graces are still acknowledged to matter, and a public-school education is definitely preferred. Elsewhere—in the civil service and much of industry—recruiters deny any automatic preference for the products of public schools. Yet public school graduates continue to do disproportionately well in the hunt for jobs. With the excellent education they receive nowadays, it would be surprising if they did not.

University education in Britain is for a minority: 12 per cent of the population, selected on the basis of their school examination results. Only seven out of a thousand people in Britain were studying for first degrees in 1982, compared with 33 out of a thousand in the United States and 19 out of a thousand in Germany. But once offered a university place, students are very unlikely to drop out. All whose parents cannot afford to support them receive a grant to cover both fees and living expenses. Facilities for studying are good, and contact with teachers is frequent and close. The result is that the percentage of graduates Britain produces out of its total population is actually higher than in most countries except the United States, Canada and Japan.

What the selection does do, of course, is to extend the advantages of those who have had the best secondary education. Ex-public school pupils made up a quarter of all university entrants in the early 1980s, and a half of the entrants to Oxford and Cambridge, the oldest and still the most prestigious of the English universities.

All is not lost, however, for those who miss out on university education at the

age of 18: Britain is well endowed with alternatives. Polytechnics offer degree courses and vocational courses, colleges of further education also have vocational courses, and the Open University, most imaginatively of all, provides undergraduate education for mature students by correspondence.

The Open University's exceptionally clear textbooks and course notes are supplemented by radio and television programmes, occasional tutorials and, for science students, home experiment kits and a week of intensive laboratory work every year. It has no age or entrance requirements, yet the standard of its degrees is as high as in other British universities—that is, high by world standards. It confers about 6,000 degrees a year—as many as Oxford and Cambridge combined.

But the Open University has not done much yet to change the traditional ratio of the classes in higher education. The overwhelming majority of its undergraduates are middle class and the biggest single group are teachers.

The British education system provides a very efficient means for the upper class and the wealthier members of the middle class to pass on their advantages to their children. But it does not follow that British society is static. Demanding jobs—both at the highest levels and at middling, white-collar levels—have multiplied in the decades since the Second World War, in Britain as in other Western countries. They are too numerous for the upper levels of society to fill entirely from within their own ranks. So new recruits have been drawn in from below at an unprecedented rate.

International surveys of mobility between manual and non-manual jobs put Britain squarely in the middle of the mobility league tables. Despite the reputation of the United States as the land of opportunity, mobility from manual to non-manual jobs over the past 20 years has been roughly the same there as it is in Britain. Denmark and Yugoslavia have similar mobility

rates, Australia and Sweden rather higher rates, and France, Germany, Italy and Spain rather lower.

Mobility into society's élite is more difficult to compare internationally than mobility between manual and non-manual jobs, because different countries and different surveys lack a universal definition of an élite. Nevertheless, the sociologist Anthony Heath has made as reliable a comparison as the data allow, and his results show that the top of British society is about as open to newcomers as the equivalent layers in France and the United States. The upper ranks of German and Italian society are rather less open than Britain's élite.

So the British, with all their preoccupations over class and rank, live in a fairly fluid society. What this paradox means is that a great many British people are busy not simply getting better jobs and spending more money but simultaneously acquiring a whole new culture—different ways of meeting friends and bringing up children, different accents, foods and hobbies. In his own lifetime a man may not complete the transition from one class to another, but it may all come easily to his children.

Brenda and Peter Hopkins are typical new recruits to Britain's middle class. Both were children of miners. They grew up in Cannock Chase in the Midlands, met at school when he was 13 and she was 12, and married seven years later. Peter failed the 11-plus examination and left school at 14 with no qualifications. He remembered his headmaster asking him if he wanted a job working with his hands or his head, and replying that either would do. It was only once he was out in the world, on an apprenticeship with the Mid-

lands Electricity Board, that he became fired with ambition. He realized that if he worked hard he could better himself, and he devoted the next 12 years to getting the education he needed. Taking day-release courses, night classes and years off for study, he qualified as a chartered engineer, sailed through a management course, and finally took a master's degree in electrical engineering.

Then promotions came fast. Peter and Brenda moved up and down the country in pursuit of the good jobs. Their present home is a spacious white stucco house near the outskirts of the pleasant cathedral city of Chester. They admit ruefully that their three children's education suffered as a consequence of all the changes of school, but feel they took the right course; many of their contemporaries who were not willing to move are still

stuck in junior positions. Now in his early forties, Peter is a senior manager on four times the national average wage. It is a level at which most managers would be happy to remain until retirement, but Peter is confident that his abilities will take him still further.

Traces of their social origins are discernible. While Peter's vowels have modified over the years, Brenda still speaks with a Midlands accent. Their furnishings reflect a working-class enthusiasm for colour, pattern and opulence. And Peter still enjoys the odd game of snooker, definitely a working-class sport.

But in other respects their lifestyle has become thoroughly middle class. Whereas in Cannock Chase they had relatives everywhere—they were the first people from their respective families to leave the town—in Chester they exist very much as a nuclear family and

do not readily mix with neighbours; they prefer to "keep themselves to themselves". They have taken up golf and they vote Conservative despite the Labour affiliations of their families. Whereas their own families took scant interest in their prospects, they have keen ambitions for their own children.

When their daughters were young, the Hopkins could not afford to send them to private schools. Neither girl did well enough at school to go to university but both subsequently got good jobs and one has married a successful young restaurateur. The Hopkins offered a private education to Mark, their youngest child, but somewhat to their regret he turned it down; he did not relish spending months of the year boarding away from his family. Mark is not an academic high-flyer like his father, but he shows great promise as a golfer and Peter would be prepared, if

Mark needed the capital to launch himself on a career as a professional golfer, to sell the house and live in a flat.

Couples like the Hopkins make up a very substantial proportion of British society: two out of every three middle-class men today were not born into the middle class. At the top of society, too, there are changes. In the 1960s, "life peerages"—peerages that could not be passed on to their holders' offspring— began to be conferred. The businessmen and trade unionists who have since swelled the ranks of the House of Lords are a very different breed from the hereditary aristocrats. Many observers of Britain are convinced that with so much movement and mixing, so many new men at the top, the days of the British preoccupation with the gradations of class are numbered. They predict that the working class and the upper class will disappear, leaving Britain an

essentially middle-class society.

They will probably be proved right in the long run, but the change may take longer than they think. The demise of class in Britain has been proclaimed many times in the past few decades, and each time the old attitudes have proved resilient.

In the late 1940s, for example, the setting up of the Welfare State—a comprehensive system of state benefits—was expected to eliminate poverty and with it class. The lot of the working man did indeed improve, but his values and loyalties remained almost untouched. Then the explosion of pop culture in the swinging Sixties momentarily made class seem irrelevant: age was what mattered, and the youth of every class was in the ascendant. Later, hope was pinned on the comprehensive schools, and in the early 1980s, much attention was devoted to the slackening of traditional class loyalties to political parties. The 1979 and 1983 General Elections were won by the Conservatives and on both occasions the biggest factor in their success was the desertion of the Labour Party by the more affluent, home-owning members of the working class.

Yet none of these changes has fundamentally altered British society. Britain's working class retains its sense of separateness; Britain still has its public schools and House of Lords. As long as these institutions endure, the British will remain something other than a homogeneous middle-class society. Easy mobility from one class to another is not in itself destined to destroy the class edifice. Indeed, the durability of Britain's open aristocracy suggests the opposite: while the British know they can move within the system, they show little inclination to destroy it.

A 17th-century library (*left*) graces Magdalene College, part of venerable Cambridge University. The building's classical detail contrasts with the sleek modern lines of a quadrangle at Sussex University outside Brighton (*above*), one of 29 British universities to be founded since World War II.

A lone fisherman casts his line on the
River Spey in Scotland. His bait, a
gaudy imitation fly, should provoke
any lurking salmon to snap in irritation
and impale itself on a hidden hook.
Before he can land the fish, he must
tire it out by "playing" it—repeatedly
slackening and winding in the line.

THE ENGROSSING RITUALS OF COUNTRY SPORT

Hunting, shooting and fly fishing are the traditional sports of Britain's aristocracy. Nowadays enjoyed by a broader social band, they have retained a certain cachet and are an integral part of the lifestyle of the upper classes—for those who live in the country and those who descend on it for long, gregarious weekends. To all in the know, these rural pursuits and rituals reverberate with clues to social status.

Fishing, to the upper-class mind, means angling for salmon, sea trout or brown trout in some delightful stretch of river—ideally one belonging to a friend, but otherwise expensively rented. The purists who exercise their skills in this way disdain reservoirs that are artificially stocked with captive and overweight rainbow trout, and have even less time for coarse fishing—luring such inferior species as roach and perch with maggots.

For shooting enthusiasts, grouse occupy the same elevated position as do salmon to a fisherman. Grouse are small and very fast in flight, delicious to eat, and found only on the moorlands of Scotland and northern England. To be invited to shoot grouse on August 12, the first day of the season, is the height of some men's ambitions. On an informal shoot, the participants move over the terrain in line, firing at birds as they get up. On grander occasions, the guns stand in line and birds are driven towards them by helpers known as beaters.

Hunting, to the British, means primarily the pursuit of the fox with a pack of hounds. Impeccably dressed horsemen and women gallop across the countryside, jumping walls and ditches and suffering not a few injuries as they get dislodged. The 200-odd hunts in Britain differ subtly in their style and membership; some of the smartest are those in the charge of noble families.

Anyone without a horse is not totally excluded from the pleasures of hunting: one form, beagling, requires only stout lungs and limbs. The dogs who give the sport its name are smaller cousins of foxhounds; the quarry in this case is a hare, which leads dogs and humans alike on a gruelling run. Several private schools keep beagles; keen hunting families make sure they send their offspring to a school with a first-class pack.

Led by the kennelman who cares for them, eager hounds set out for their rendezvous with the horsemen.

In hot pursuit of a fox, a hunt thunders past Alnwick Castle, the home of the Duke of Northumberland. When the fox is caught, the mask (head) and

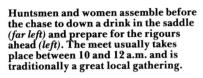

Huntsmen and women assemble before the chase to down a drink in the saddle *(far left)* and prepare for the rigours ahead *(left)*. The meet usually takes place between 10 and 12 a.m. and is traditionally a great local gathering.

brush (tail) are often presented to the first rider to arrive at the scene of the kill.

BAGGING THE BIRDS

As a man takes aim, a helper crouches beside him, poised to pass him a second gun, ready primed, so that he can fire again at the covey passing overhead. The dog waits to retrieve the fallen birds.

On the "Glorious Twelfth" of August, a man and a woman wait behind a hide or "butt" on the misty Yorkshire moors. Like other shooters manning a line of similar butts strung out about 100 metres apart, they will spring into action when the beaters, advancing towards them, raise some grouse.

Onlookers gather round the Christchurch and Farley Hill Beagles, a pack run by Oxford University undergraduates. Although the day's sport has not begun, the hunt master's once immaculate breeches have already been sullied with pawprints from an over-affectionate hound.

On the scent of a hare, the beagles stream across an Oxfordshire field. The leaders of the hunt match the dogs' pace and endeavour to keep them

CHASING THE HARE THROUGH BOG, BUSH AND BRIAR

The hunt splashes across a deeply rutted lane.

A resolute youth leaps a muddy stream.

together on the trail. Hares generally run in a circle, so by the end of the day the hunt will probably find itself back near its starting point.

4

AFTERMATH OF AN EMPIRE

The greatest empire the world has ever seen had vanished, and the British who had been its rulers had shrunk back to their native islands. Of their overseas dominions, all that remained was a scattering of awkward little dependencies, places no longer useful but too small to have independence thrust upon them. None, apparently, had any influence on British policies. Then, in April 1982, the troops of the military government of Argentina invaded the Falkland Islands.

The Argentinians had long laid claim to the Malvinas, as they called the islands: quite apart from legal arguments, they were 13,000 kilometres from London and only 650 from Argentina. The islands were virtually worthless and their distance from London meant recapture could be expensive and risky. The Junta in Buenos Aires was entirely confident that its surprise attack would result in grudging British acceptance of a *fait accompli*.

Instead, the invasion triggered in Britain a ferocious and immediate response to what was felt to be a national humiliation. Prime Minister Margaret Thatcher ordered the fleet to sea and battle began. Ten weeks later, the Union Jack flew once more over the tiny colonial capital of Port Stanley. The fighting had cost Britain 1,000 casualties, as well as several billion pounds' worth of ships and aircraft; but even as the losses mounted, the Prime Minister's popularity climbed. During the summer of 1982, as the ships of Britain's task force came home to a joyous welcome, national morale was higher than it had been for decades.

The majority of the British people felt that there was no choice but to retaliate to the Argentine invasion: they had a duty towards the Falkland islanders, who wished to remain British. But beneath that logic lurked nostalgia for a golden age. The vanishing of the Empire in the decades after World War II coincided for Britain with a sharp drop in status and power, and in wealth relative to that of other nations. Most historians now agree that the British Empire was a result and not a cause of Britain's former greatness; in cold economic terms, Britons are better off without their far-reaching responsibilities. But the Empire had offered the most visible and glorious evidence of the standing that Britain used to enjoy in the world, and the invitation to relive its pride and pomp proved irresistible.

The British Empire was an astonishing creation—if anything can be called a creation that arose with so little formal planning. It began with the aggressive forays of 16th-century seafarers, men like Sir Francis Drake and Sir John Hawkins, who were distinguishable from common pirates only by royal favour and a certain sense of style. It was first extended by emigration across the Atlantic, so that by the middle of the 18th century Britain held sway over

The aircraft carrier *Invincible* sails home to a tumultuous reception after taking part in the 1982 campaign to recapture the Falkland Islands from Argentina. The Falklands war, fought some 13,000 kilometres from Britain's shores, evoked the greatest outpouring of patriotic fervour since World War II.

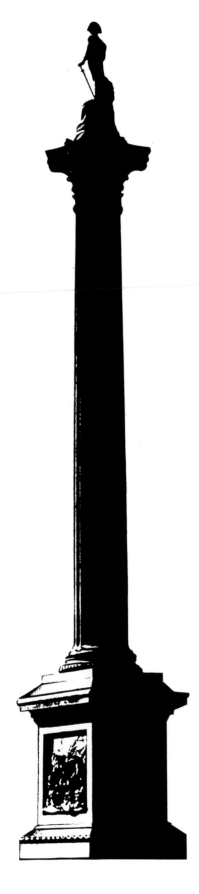

the entire eastern seaboard of North America from Hudson Bay to Georgia. It attained its greatest extent in 1933, when it embraced a quarter of the earth's land surface and at least a quarter of its people. Essentially, though, it was a 19th-century phenomenon, the manifestation of British industrial might and the moral self-confidence of Victorian England.

Seapower was the key to empire. During more than 20 years of war—from 1793 to 1815—with revolutionary and then Napoleonic France, the Royal Navy was Britain's first and, at times, only defence against overwhelming continental armies, commanding a huge proportion of the nation's resources. By the time the wars ended, the Royal Navy had no rival anywhere. For the next century, the oceans of the world were close to being a British lake.

Wealth fuelled the reach for territories. Until the end of the 18th century, Britain had been merely a farming and trading nation, albeit a successful one. By the 1780s, Britain had plunged into the world's first industrial revolution. Steam, coal and iron transformed Britain into the workshop of the world and the richest country on earth, ready to exploit any market it could reach.

The precepts of evangelical Christianity offered another powerful motive for empire-building. The 19th century saw a religious revival in Britain and the idea that an empire had a duty of trusteeship to its peoples. For the 19th-century imperialists, the Empire was less a matter of national interest than a great engine for the progress of humanity: by extending its dominions, they were discharging an obligation laid upon them by Almighty God.

In the Victorian era, many British people came in a quiet way to think of

themselves as a master race; and certainly they had a good deal to feel masterful about. The world maps hanging in every British schoolroom blazed with imperial pink. Because the territories girdled the globe, it was proudly noted that the sun never set on the British Empire—even if, as cynics added, that simply meant that the Good Lord dared not trust the British in the dark.

On the ground, the Empire was far more heterogeneous than the uniform pink suggested. The American colonies had revolted and left the Empire in 1776, but there were still the white Dominions: Canada and Australia, South Africa and New Zealand, very British in lifestyle and attitudes and enjoying virtually total independence while professing allegiance to the British crown. Then there was India, hugely populous, ruled by a tiny British élite who talked of bringing the subcontinent to the status of an independent Dominion in some indeterminate future.

India herself had been a major cause of further expansion. To protect the route to the subcontinent, Britain took Cape Colony—the germ of the future South Africa—from the Dutch in 1795. After the Suez Canal was opened in 1869, Indian security required a British presence in Egypt, the Red Sea and the Persian Gulf. To keep an eye on Egypt meant controlling the Eastern Mediterranean, for which the acquisition of Cyprus provided a convenient base. Eastwards, too, Indian defence demanded the absorption of Burma and at least encouraged the annexation of the rest of Britain's Far Eastern Empire, including Malaya, whose rubber plantations made it the most profitable of all imperial possessions.

In Africa there were three different British Empires: South Africa, of

From a massive Corinthian column, Admiral Lord Nelson gazes over London's Trafalgar Square, named after the sea battle of 1805 in which he died. The battle crushed the fleets of Napoleon and confirmed Britain as the world's leading naval power.

A decorative map, printed in 1902 for the coronation of Edward VII, shows the British Empire coloured pink. At the top, the British lion radiates light over the national animals of his far-flung domain. The royal emblems of a lion and a unicorn *(below)* support the arms of 18 colonies and dependencies.

course; then East and Central Africa, where a few thousand British settlers had staked out prosperous farms in tribal lands. In West Africa there were no settlers. Instead, a handful of imperial officials brought as much law and order as their budgets would allow to vast and scarcely surveyed regions.

And then there was the small change of empire: a naval base here, a coaling station there, and islands—including the windswept, forgotten Falklands—just about everywhere. How these oddments had first come under the British flag, few could remember for sure. Some of them—the West Indies, for example—had been British since the 17th century; others—the barren rock of Ascension Island, say, or little St. Helena—had been annexed by passing naval officers more or less from force of habit; others still—most notably the island chain of Fiji—had been received into the Empire at their own request, usually grudgingly, since the Treasury in London was always complaining about the expense.

No part of the Empire was typical of the whole, and the possession about which the British felt most keenly was perhaps the most exceptional of all. It was the massive subcontinent of India, with its ancient cultures and complexities, that was conjured up in the average British mind by the mention of Empire. They called it "the jewel in the crown", and when Queen Victoria allowed herself to be proclaimed an imperial monarch, the title she accepted was "Empress of India".

When Britain expelled the French from India in the 18th century, it had been largely as a side-effect of European conflict and the object had been no more than to ensure the continuation of Britain's lucrative Indian trade:

4

the idea of governing the tumultuous subcontinent horrified most thinking men in London. But the merchant-adventurers of the East India Company were less inhibited. Using a skilful mixture of diplomacy and brute force, they expanded into the power vacuum that had existed since the collapse of the Moghul Empire a century before. In vain, the British Government—chary of so vast a responsibility—urged restraint. By 1833, the Company's trading function had disappeared and it became a governing agency, to all intents and purposes an arm of British power. Even so, it was only after the Indian Mutiny of 1857—when a large part of the Company's native troops rose up in a brief rebellion, bloodily suppressed—that the British Government overcame its reluctance to assume formal control.

In the early days of the East India Company, administration was rough and ready. Officials were paid little, although not many complained: the few who survived fever and warfare generally managed to return to Britain with enough booty to ensure a comfortable retirement. By the 1830s, though, attitudes had changed, and the Indian civil service was born. It was to serve as a model for the administration of the entire Empire and eventually, in 1870, when the British civil service was redesigned, for Britain itself.

The ICS did not acquire its official title until 1853, but it was conceived from the beginning as an élite organization, highly paid and selected by competitive examination at a time when appointments in Britain's own civil service were arranged by patronage and bribery. More remarkably still, successful candidates for the ICS—whose previous education had consisted mainly of Greek and Latin—had to spend two years learning Indian languages before they took up their posts. But the most startling aspect of the ICS was its size—or lack of it. Throughout the 19th century, there were never more than a thousand of these mandarins. Between them, they governed 300 million people.

Of course, each mandarin represented the top of a pyramid whose base was provided by highly trained Indian clerks. Nevertheless, the power delegated to a member of the ICS was awesome. A young man not long from England might find himself administering a district with a population of half a million. He would see few other British people socially and—given the huge distances involved—he rarely had the opportunity to refer problems to superiors. He had to take the responsibility for his own decisions and suffer the consequences of his own mistakes.

Nor could he rely heavily on military force to back up an unpopular ruling. British imperial rule did not depend on large armies. There were rarely more than 40,000 British troops in all India—at one point during World War I the number dropped to 15,000—and the Indian Army, recruited mainly from the warrior races of the Punjab, was generally only about 170,000.

The British writer and historian Philip Mason, who joined the ICS in the 1920s, remembers what it was like to keep the peace with those minimal forces: "It was a remarkable feat, an extraordinary bluff, really, that such a very small number of us could hold the country. But it was only possible because we were responsive to the people we governed. We did listen to what people said. The received idea today is that the rule of one people over another is obviously immoral; I think it can sometimes be a good thing. The Roman Empire in France, for example: most Frenchmen would agree it was a good thing, although there were some pretty nasty things done in the course of it. I think it's a matter of what the intention is, and how long you mean it to last. The power you exercise is one of trusteeship. All of us thought of British rule as something transitory."

But while the members of the ICS, schooled in a liberal tradition of service, foresaw and reconciled themselves to the end of Empire, many others were arrogant enough to believe that the British were indispensable to their subjects and that their global rule would last forever. Even the clearer-sighted failed to realize how rapidly the end would come.

In 1897, the year of the ceremonies which celebrated Queen Victoria's Diamond Jubilee, the poet Rudyard Kipling had written:

Far-called, our navies melt away;
On dune and headland sinks the fire:
Lo, all our pomp of yesterday
Is one with Nineveh and Tyre.

The poem raised the hairs on the back of many an imperial neck—but only in a gentle way, of course, since its prophecy clearly belonged to the far, far future. That future, in fact, was not so distant. In exactly 50 years, India would escape Britain's guardianship; and the rest of the Empire would disappear, like mist in the sunshine, a few decades after that.

The 20th century has not been kind to Britain and its Empire. Beginning in the 1870s, Britain's position as the greatest industrial producer was suc-

A scout from Gambia proudly wears his troop's headgear, khaki shirt and neckerchief. Founded in 1907 by Lord Baden-Powell, a distinguished soldier, the movement has developed from a brotherhood of the British Empire into a worldwide youth fraternity of over 16 million members.

cessfully challenged both by Germany and the United States; and although in 1914 it was still the wealthiest nation in the world, it was increasingly dependent upon income from investments rather than from manufacturing output. Victory in World War I was bought at a colossal price—in treasure as well as blood. At the end of the conflict, Britain was somewhat in the position of an elderly lady with a vast, rambling mansion on her hands and a drastically reduced income to pay for the increasing costs of upkeep.

On the surface, the war was a triumphant demonstration of the Empire's strength and unity. Young men from the white Dominions streamed across the oceans to fight and die for the Mother Country. India stayed loyal. The Indian army sent reinforcements to France at a vital moment and furnished troops for Middle East campaigns. Victory even added to the imperial territory: most of Germany's colonies and several provinces of the Ottoman Empire became mandates of the new League of Nations and came under British administrative control.

But it was becoming clear that the expense of running the global agglomeration for which Britain was responsible far exceeded the capability of an economy that was no longer in the world's first rank. Fervent 19th-century imperialists had regarded the Empire as the source of British strength. Now men began to realize that the opposite was true. The Empire had been the outward sign of Britain's wealth, an effect and not a cause, and as the wealth declined, so would the Empire that the wealth had won.

In fact, the importance of the Empire had always been more symbolic than real, more moral than economic. Capi-

4

talist imperialists, at least according to the ideas of the 1980s, are supposed to be exploiters: their dominions provide them with huge captive markets and guarantee them cheap raw materials. And it is true that the Empire provided an important market for British manufactured goods and Britain, in turn, came to rely heavily on imports of food from the Empire. Yet throughout the imperial era, most British trade was with Europe and America. In 1913, for example, the whole of Asia provided only 13 per cent of British imports, and British overseas investments followed a similar pattern. Most of the Empire

was underdeveloped and unindustrialized. British capitalists preferred to put their money into the U.S. South America also appealed to them more than Africa or Asia: it is ironic, in view of later events, that by 1914 Britain had invested almost as much capital in Argentina alone as it had in all India.

Even in terms of emigration, the Empire had been far less important to the British than imperialists liked to imagine at the time. Between 1815 and 1914, some 20 million people—almost half of Britain's 1914 population—left to seek a new life overseas. Of these, fully two thirds turned their backs on

all things British and settled in the U.S. Those who stayed at home thought fondly of the other one third who remained within the Empire as part of a global British family. But while the emigrants often shared their sentimentality, they cherished even more stoutly their new-found independence.

After World War I, the practical consequences of that independence became inescapable. In the 1920s, the British made attempts to create from the Empire a meaningful economic and political federation, but each effort foundered on the understandable determination of Canada, South Africa,

Australia, New Zealand—and, from 1922, the newest of the Dominions, the Irish Free State—to preserve their own freedom of action. In place of a working federation, London had to settle for the promulgation of the "British Commonwealth of Nations", defined by the Statute of Westminster in 1931 as a free association of autonomous communities, none subordinate to any other.

Throughout the 1930s, the rest of the Empire creaked steadily on, much as before, despite the parlous state of imperial finances and the war clouds looming in Europe. India was clamouring for independence: for more than 150 years the British had seen themselves as trustees for the Indian people, but now that their wards were declaring themselves of age the trustees showed a definite reluctance to depart. Elsewhere, too, in Burma and Malaya, there were stirrings of nationalism.

Worst of all, the emergence of imperial Japan as a voracious military rival in the Far East presented the British Empire with an external threat against which it was virtually defenceless. When that threat became a conquering reality in 1941, war in Europe had put Britain into such dire straits that collapse in the East was inevitable.

All wars are disastrous, but the Second World War was more disastrous than most. The British had their moment of heroism, standing alone against Hitler; but without the United States and the Soviet Union as allies they could never have triumphed. In a laconic summary of each partner's contribution, Stalin said, "Great Britain provided time; the United States provided money; and Soviet Russia provided blood." The cost of the time that Britain gave the world was its own extinction as an independent great power—and the consequent destruction of the British Empire.

On the surface, Britain's exhaustion after the war was not obvious. Though its cities were somewhat scarred, its territory remained intact: the Far Eastern colonies overrun by Japan had been recovered. But its economy, distorted by war production and bereft for the war years of the export markets where it earned a living, could barely support its own people. In time, the economy would recover. What was lost beyond recovery was the will to rule.

For years in India the British had haggled with native politicians over independence terms, hoping against hope that Muslim and Hindu could live together in a unitary state after their departure. Progress had been agonizingly slow, for the British had stalled again and again. Some of them had persisted in the belief that Indians would not be fit to manage their own affairs for decades to come; even those free from such patronizing attitudes had been in no great hurry to lose their most glorious imperial possession. Now, the British had had enough. In 1947 they presented an ultimatum: they were going, partition or no partition. Amid horrific scenes of communal violence, India and Pakistan emerged as independent nations. After 200 years, the British Raj was over.

Once India had gone, the rest of the Empire followed it into independence. By now, few in Britain doubted the necessity and wisdom of such a policy: the surprise was the speed with which it came to pass. Even the 1945 Labour Government, by no means enthusiastically imperialist, had envisaged a long period of tutelage for the embryo nations in its care, especially in Africa: it greatly increased the recruitment of career administrators for its colonies. But nationalism was also at work in Africa and, not without misgivings, the British granted independence to Ghana in 1957 and Nigeria in 1960.

The next decade saw the last and in some ways most frenetic stage in the Empire's history: it became a factory dedicated to the production of brand-new nation-states. Other colonial empires were breaking up, but none on the same scale as the British, or with quite as much style. A glittering imperial roadshow, headed by a token member of the British royal family, whirled around the world granting independence apparently to anyone who asked for it; at the time, it seemed as if new countries were created almost weekly.

Sometimes the gift turned out to be a poisoned chalice. More than one ex-colony has since discovered that self-government does not necessarily mean good government, that law and order are not so easily achieved as their former overlords had sometimes made it seem, and that the *pax Britannica*, for all its faults, at least had been a *pax*. The wars between India and Pakistan in 1965 and 1971, the civil wars in Cyprus and Nigeria in the 1960s and Uganda in the 1970s, the racial conflicts in Sri Lanka in the 1980s all show in a sadly negative way the skill the British once had used to keep the peace (or, as some have cynically claimed, their skill at choosing the right moment to depart). But staying on, unwanted, had never been a serious British option. Neither British nor world opinion would have stood for it, and the movement towards independence was inexorable.

In general, the British have accepted the end of the old order with a good grace. They take comfort from the

BRITAIN TOASTS THE QUEEN

It was, said Prince Philip, "a good excuse for a party". For seven days in June 1977, virtually the whole of Britain erupted in exuberant celebration of Queen Elizabeth II's Silver Jubilee—the 25th anniversary of her accession to the throne. Determined not only to show their affection for the monarch but to enjoy themselves into the bargain, the British embarked on a rare and spectacular round of carnivals, processions, pageants, firework displays and open-air parties.

The ceremonial highlight occurred on the first day, when the Queen rode in her gilded state coach from Buckingham Palace to St. Paul's Cathedral for a thanksgiving service. But the keynote of the week was informality, and it was in the obscure side-streets, with their festoons of flags, bunting and royal portraits, that the festivities were mainly focused. In London alone there were 5,000 street parties, as well as 2,000 other events ranging from poetry reading to bicycle races.

Swept along by the tide of national euphoria, many people adorned their pets, their cars and themselves in a variety of patriotic regalia. Some went so far as to dye their hair in red, white and blue stripes.

Everyone, it seemed, was anxious to join in. In one affluent London borough, for instance, a policeman sprouting two Union Jacks from his helmet led a conga line of 300 residents—including four members of Parliament and several diplomats. Nor was Jubilee fever confined to the natives. An Hawaiian based in Suffolk with the U.S. Air Force gave his daughter a name which meant "Jessica the heavenly beauty who loves England and was born in the year of the Queen's Jubilee".

A jubilee window display comes in for some critical scrutiny.

Fashion reaches new heights with a Tower of London hat.

A patriotically clad citizen poses before his decorated home.

indirect influence they still exert in the world through two flourishing native products—their language and their institutions of government.

Six hundred years ago, the English language was a bastard dialect of Norman French and Anglo-Saxon, understood by no more than a few hundred thousand people. Today, only Mandarin is spoken by more people, and students throughout the world struggle to learn English as the international language of science, business and politics. The British tradition of parliamentary government has provided the constitutional model for a large part of the free world and the Common Law of England has furnished scores of nations with the foundations of their legal system.

And there is still the Commonwealth to boost the British sense of being at the centre of something, although it has dropped the prefix "British" and changed out of all recognition since its inauguration in 1931. Then, it was a club of six culturally and ethnically homogeneous nations. Of its founder members, Ireland seceded in 1949 and South Africa in 1961, but most former British colonies joined up willingly on independence, and now it is a loose association of 48 states, ranging in size and prosperity from tiny republics under Marxist rule—for example, the Seychelles—to the affluent consumer societies of Canada and Australia.

As a result, the member-states have few things in common, and wealth is not one of them. Since it has no political unity, the Commonwealth has no political power; but it functions very well as an information exchange and a channel by which aid can flow from richer to poorer countries. The Commonwealth is certainly not an instrument of British policy: in theory, at least, the British could be expelled from their own club. But in a quiet way it is a force that works towards world harmony.

The most important of Britain's relationships with its former colonies, however, has nothing to do with the Commonwealth. The United States of America left the Empire the hard way more than 200 years ago, after inflicting on Britain one of the most ignominious defeats in its history. In time, the bitterness caused by the American War of Independence faded and there grew up between the two countries a love-hate relationship that has persisted to the present day. The ties between the two are strong: a common language, a common history and a good deal of straightforward blood kinship. In view of these links, the British government has long laid claim to what it calls a "special relationship" with the United States. The idea has been a comfort to the British in their period of rapidly declining power and a source of irritation to other nations: the French, for example, sometimes grumble darkly about *"la conspiration anglo-saxonne"*.

In fact, the special relationship is a delicate one and has certainly never reached the status of a conspiracy. In the 19th century, when Britain was by far the stronger of the two powers, relations were often strained; indeed, in 1812, the two countries were at war with each other. A century later, when Britain was embroiled in the carnage of World War I, the Americans wisely took care to stay neutral for as long as possible. Afterwards they rejected British proposals for a naval alliance in the Far East that would have greatly eased the burdens of the Royal Navy.

The Second World War and its aftermath put new strains on the special relationship. For the first time, Britain could not survive without American aid. Yet a residual fear of Britain as a trading rival ensured that U.S. Lend-Lease aid supplied to Britain to fund the war was given on terms that crippled Britain's export industries. No such conditions hedged the aid the U.S. sent its other ally—the Soviet Union.

The Suez crisis of 1956 brought the special relationship to its lowest ebb. It came about when British and French troops, acting in collusion with Israeli forces, attempted to take over the Suez Canal, newly nationalized by Egypt. The U.S., outraged at this last imperial fling, not only refused to support the British action but also threatened financially ruinous countermeasures unless Britain withdrew.

Humiliated, the British government backed down. The Suez adventure had been, at best, a blunder and at worst the most shameful episode in recent British history. Objectively it is hard to fault U.S. policy: many in Britain had denounced the action. But many others felt betrayed by Britain's greatest ally.

Nevertheless, Britain remains the staunchest of America's European partners and a committed member of NATO. Even if the old idea of kinship is fading, the special relationship continues to exist.

At home, the most visible and probably the most durable legacy of empire is the sight of the black and brown faces in Britain's cities. In a way, it is ironic: in the high days of empire, no more than a minute fraction of the 400 million or so Africans and Asians who were officially British subjects ever visited the British Isles; but as the Empire began to dwindle, a flood of immigrants from the new Commonwealth countries—mainly from the West Indies, India

WINNING THE WAR ON THE HOME FRONT

For Britain, the darkest period of World War II began in the summer of 1940 with Hitler's lightning sweep through France to the Channel coast. From then until the following June, when the Führer launched his fateful attack on the Soviet Union, the British stood alone against the relentless fury of the Nazi air force. London was bombed every night for two months; several other cities were also badly hit. Many children were evacuated to the country, but most city dwellers stayed put and managed as best they could.

The common threat brought a sense of unity to the British people, and everyone became engaged in the struggle to win the war. Women, for example, were suddenly thrust into the centre of the industrial stage. The call-up of men was denuding factories of labour, so the government decided to conscript women. No other nation—not even the two great monoliths of Germany or the Soviet Union—was prepared to go that far. Female conscription not only helped to revitalize British war production, but also gave many women their first glimpse of a world beyond the kitchen sink.

For the thousands of men either too old or too young to join the regular forces, there existed the Local Defence Volunteers, later called the Home Guard. Deployed to watch over such targets as aerodromes, factories and public utilities, this part-time militia was particularly popular with ex-servicemen.

A less arduous outlet for patriotic proclivities was provided by the vast network of social groups aiding the war-effort, such as pig-breeding clubs and knitting circles. With British ships under constant attack, such groups helped to make up the shortfall in imports of food and clothing. Schools played their own part in the drive for balaclavas and bacon rashers, and some even geared themselves up for the production of aircraft components. As the historian A.J.P. Taylor has observed, "The war was a people's war in the most literal sense."

A veteran responds to the appeal for knitwear.

Bombed-out office staff carry on as normal.

Women railway workers turn out a batch of concrete sleepers.

Schoolboys join a production line.

Hyde Park police display a prize beast from their piggery. With food shortages, many Londoners became part-time breeders.

Children on a London housing estate help prepare sandbags as a precaution against air attacks.

4

and Pakistan—sought their fortunes in the old Imperial "homeland".

The timing of Commonwealth immigration, in fact, had little to do with imperial politics and everything to do with the economic boom that Britain, like other Western nations, experienced in the 1950s and 60s. Faced with a labour shortage, British employers turned to their colonies and ex-colonies for a supply of workers likely to settle for the low-paid jobs that were most on offer. For a nation that has seen no influx of comparable size since the Norman Conquest in 1066, the social strains have been considerable.

Even in boom times there were difficulties. At first, the British government was unwilling to impede immigration, partly because labour was needed and partly because to do so would have been out of keeping with the new idea of the Commonwealth and its implication that a quarter of the world was British, after a fashion. Anti-immigrant riots in London in 1958 shocked liberal British opinion but made immigration control a vote-catching issue, and in the 1960s governments of each major party imposed increasingly restrictive Immigration Acts. To compensate, further legislation outlawed racial discrimination in housing and employment; in 1968 Home Secretary Roy Jenkins proudly announced that Britain had become a "multicultural society".

On one level it was true enough. Most British cities now had areas where Afro-Asian faces seemed to predominate, strange music filled the air, and shops and restaurants sold exotic foods. But the first signs of economic recession were beginning to appear, and the anti-discrimination laws were weak and difficult to enforce. Immigrants who had come to Britain full of hope

looked at the bleak prospect and bitterly began to use the word "ghetto".

By the late 1970s the black population had reached 1.9 million—3.5 per cent of the total population. Although half of the 1.9 million were born in Britain, most lived in the poorest quarters of the inner cities. Unemployment was rising fast. Relations between the almost entirely white police force and young blacks—especially young West Indians, among whom unemployment figures had reached horrendous proportions—were bad and getting worse. In April 1981, tensions exploded in the worst riots Britain had seen for 200 years. Fires blazed in London and several other major cities. The multicultural society seemed in ruins.

Yet there were redeeming factors. The riots did not follow the black versus white pattern of 1958. Instead, it was young blacks—usually assisted by young whites, who were also enduring high levels of unemployment—against the police. For their part, the police fought back without the use of firearms.

As a way of airing a grievance, the riots were expensive, but they were not entirely ineffective. A dismayed police force made efforts to recruit more men and women from the ethnic minorities, and painfully reappraised its tactics—not only for fighting the riots but for avoiding them in the first place. More government money was made available to help ease inner-city problems; and some local authorities in areas with high black populations began limited programmes of positive discrimination in employment.

In the vital area of education, commitment to the idea of the multicultural society, despite its setbacks, is as strong as ever. The easy optimism of the 1960s has gone, however. A senior

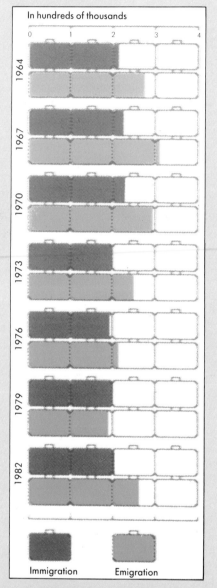

ARRIVALS AND DEPARTURES

In hundreds of thousands

1964
1967
1970
1973
1976
1979
1982

Immigration   Emigration

Large-scale immigration to Britain began in the 1950s with an influx of newcomers from the countries of the Commonwealth, and peaked in the late 1960s. In 1981, immigrants made up 6.3 per cent of the British population, a slightly lower figure than in France, the Netherlands or West Germany. About half the immigrants are from the West Indies, India, Pakistan and Bangladesh. The others are from a variety of countries, including Australia, the U.S., Spain and Italy. Since the early 1950s, emigration has almost always exceeded immigration.

English teacher in a North London school put it this way: "We used to announce, 'I don't know what colour the children in my class are,' and feel proud of ourselves for treating race as if it were irrelevant. It took a long time to realize that we were being stupid, even insulting. In fact, it's essential to take a child's cultural background into account. What language do they speak at home? What are their parents' attitudes? They're all individuals, and you have to treat them that way."

Her school's intake is roughly one third West Indian and African; Asians, Greeks and Turks—from Cyprus, once a British colony—make up another third. Such labels are of course misleading, since most are British-born; but the wide range of backgrounds puts severe demands on a teacher.

"You have to use the differences, not ignore them: get the kids to tell stories in their own dialects, let them learn a little of each other's languages. That way, you can let a child take pride in his background. At the same time you can make the whole class see the importance of standard English."

Traditional syllabuses have been modified to take account of ethnic differences; outside the classroom, many teachers attend racism awareness courses to help them understand, and thus eliminate, their own unconscious prejudices. But the world beyond the schools is still a harsh place for Britain's minorities, and the long-term effect of a determinedly liberal educational policy remains to be seen.

Imperfectly but irreversibly, most British people are learning to accept that it is possible to be British and black. Since 1973, when Britain joined the European Economic Community, they have also had to accept that it is necessary to be British and European.

Geographically, of course, they always have been. Politically too, Britain is, was, and always will be a European power, inevitably involved in European conflicts and sharing Europe's general destiny. Emotionally, though, the British have never been anything but deeply ambivalent towards the continent. The sea around their islands was a bulwark against invasion long before it became the highway to the Empire, and Shakespeare accurately summed up Britons' feelings about their island when he wrote of it as:

. . . this little world,
This precious stone set in the silver sea,
Which serves it in the office of a wall,
Or as a moat defensive to a house,
Against the envy of less happier lands.

The 19th-century Empire allowed Britain to turn its back on Europe with impunity; the 20th-century Empire deluded Britain into imagining it could do the same. Yet paradoxically, Britain was one of the earliest proponents of European union. In a speech in 1946, the former prime minister Winston Churchill called for the establishment of a European version of the U.S. His plan, however, did not envisage Britain as a member: with their world empire, the British had bigger fish to fry.

Later, still imagining themselves to be a world power and absorbed in the transformation of the Empire into the Commonwealth, the British watched benevolently from the sidelines as France, Germany, Italy and the Benelux countries negotiated their way towards the Treaty of Rome, which established the EEC in 1957. It was only when the British began to notice the prosperity that the EEC was generating—and then compared it to their own much poorer economic performance—that they realized they had made a mistake. By then, it was too late. Throughout the 1960s, repeated applications for membership were rebuffed by the veto of France's General de Gaulle; finally, in 1973, the British were allowed to participate.

Unfortunately, the EEC they joined was not the EEC that they had hoped to join. The breathtaking expansion of the 1960s was over; energy crises and recession lay ahead, and the great ideals of European unity faded somewhat amid the endless bickering that the slump encouraged.

The British bickered more than the others. They felt they paid a disproportionate amount towards the upkeep of the vast bureaucracy in Brussels and there was some justice in their complaints. There was also justice in the complaints of Britain's partners that British commitment to the community was less than wholehearted. Parochialism had proved hard to overcome. That deep ambivalence remained.

But although their hearts have not been won, the British people have shown themselves committed to Europe by their heads: in cold logic, they know they have no place else to go. Despite a definite lack of public enthusiasm for the EEC, a referendum held in 1975 confirmed British membership by a majority of two to one.

In retrospect, British expectations from the EEC were absurdly high. They are more realistic now. No one imagines the Community is going to cure Britain's chronic post-war industrial malaise unaided. But most agree that the future, for better or worse, must lie with Europe. The days of empire will not come back.

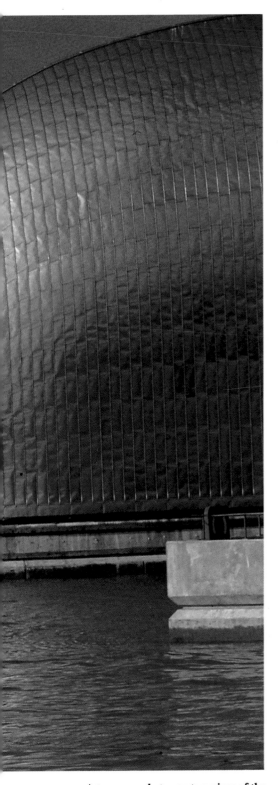

A tug passes between two piers of the Thames Flood Barrier—the largest moveable flood barrier in the world, and a sophisticated example of British engineering. Minutes after learning of a high tide that threatens London, operators can raise huge steel gates in position between the piers.

AN ECONOMY IN TRANSITION

In recent years, much concern has been expressed over the state of the British economy, especially in Britain itself. Gloom, doom and national decay are favourite topics in the nation's bars, and sometimes it seems that one of the country's principal growth industries is the publication of books on the theme of what went wrong and how much worse things can be expected to get. Yet, while it is easy to produce evidence of crisis, a sanguine interpretation of Britain's economic state can seem equally plausible. It all depends on what evidence you pick.

Optimists can point, first of all, to Britain's rapid adjustment to membership of the European Economic Community. Within a few years of joining the EEC in 1973, Britain exchanged its traditional dependence on trade with the countries of the former Empire and the underdeveloped world—in which it called most of the shots—for a deep involvement with the countries of Europe, many of which had been its traditional adversaries. Twenty-nine per cent of British exports went to the EEC in 1970, 43 per cent a decade later. Meanwhile, British manufacturers switched from Empire to European raw materials—from Mauritian sugar cane, for example, to French sugar beet. The transition was managed with surprising ease.

Equally positive has been the discovery and exploration of North Sea oil, one of the most difficult and challenging engineering tasks ever undertaken anywhere in the world. It is easy to forget, now that the oil has been flowing for a number of years, just how astonishing the achievement has been. Oil had never been recovered from waters as deep as those in the North Sea. Nor had it been exploited from fields situated so far offshore, nor in seas where the weather was so bad and the weather windows—the spells of good weather, measured in mere days a year—were so short.

When the oil was discovered, in 1969, Britain had no experience of the sort of offshore engineering that would be needed to extract it. In the early years, British companies supplied only a quarter of the equipment and services required in the North Sea. A decade later, they had augmented their share of this lucrative market to three quarters, and they were increasingly involved in supplying offshore oil markets around the world. In the 1980s, Britain had become the world's fifth largest oil producer and one of the few industrial countries self-sufficient in the fuel. In addition, the North Sea supplies the nation with enough natural gas to meet the major part of its gas requirements for decades.

Yet another credit in the national balance-sheet is the cybernetic revolution; British families have been bringing computers into their homes at a faster rate than any other nation. The boom is a tribute to the British inventor

113

5

Sir Clive Sinclair; the tiny machines he developed brought computers within the price range of the mass market for the first time. Partly as an offshoot of his efforts, Britain also now has a vigorous software industry.

In more traditional fields too, parts at least of the British economy justify optimism. Britain has a dozen or so multinational companies as successful as any of their foreign equivalents. Besides British Petroleum (BP) and the predominantly British Shell group—the only major oil companies outside the United States—the market leaders include the British-American Tobacco (BAT) group, the largest non-American employer in the United States, with interests ranging from cosmetics to insurance as well as cigarettes; and Imperial Chemical Industries (ICI), one of the world's foremost chemical companies; and General Electric, a leading producer of electrical goods. The service sector of the economy remains healthy; the facilities provided in the City of London by banks, insurance companies and fund managers maintain the capital's long-held position as the world's financial centre. And in agriculture too, the British continue a lengthy tradition of excellence. With less than 3 per cent of the population employed on the land—a minute proportion compared with Germany's 6 per cent, France's 8 per cent and Italy's 11 per cent—the British produce more than half the food they need to feed themselves. Their farms are models of efficiency, careful husbandry and intelligent use of capital.

For the pessimists, however, even these bright spots fail to provide much cheer. They point out that the North Sea oil bonanza will continue for only two or three decades, and that while it

AN ABUNDANCE OF ENERGY

Britain is better endowed with energy resources than any other nation in Western Europe. The extensive coalfields of north and central England, south Wales, and the Scottish Lowlands have been exploited since the 18th century, but reserves remain for another 300 years. Gas and high-quality, light oil discovered in the 1960s have made Britain self-sufficient in energy in net terms. Small sources of oil and gas have been found on land but major fields are offshore—in the northern North Sea for oil, in the southern North Sea for gas. More than half the oil is exported; the remainder meets a quarter of the nation's own energy needs. Gas from Britain's sector of the North Sea provides a further one sixth of the energy consumed in Britain. The oil and gas are expected to last a few decades into the 21st century.

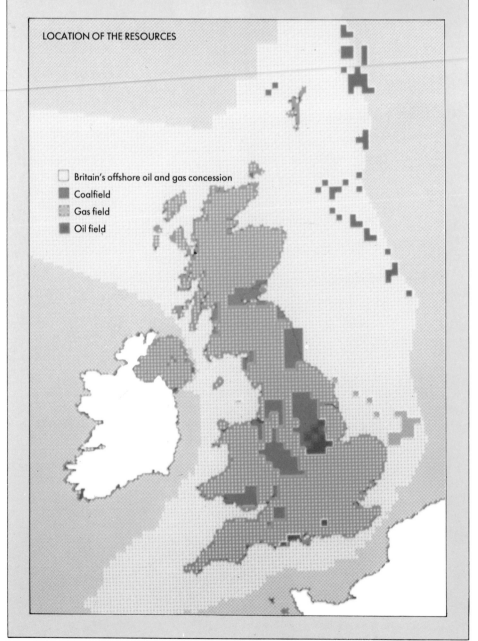

LOCATION OF THE RESOURCES

☐ Britain's offshore oil and gas concession
■ Coalfield
▒ Gas field
■ Oil field

lasts it tempts the British to relax and enjoy a false sense of security instead of striving to create more industry. They note that computer technology is an unpredictable and highly risky business, in which Britain is by no means certain of retaining an important share. They observe that farmers have only managed to achieve their phenomenal productivity through massive government subsidies which might have been better used elsewhere. Above all, they argue that all the positive aspects of the British economy cannot compensate for its glaring weakness, a shaky manufacturing base.

British manufacturing has been decimated in the past few years. Between 1970 and 1980, the work force in the steel, shipbuilding, textile and coal-mining industries dropped by between a quarter and two thirds. The onset of the world recession in the late 1970s brought further contraction and unemployment levels not seen since the Depression of the 1930s. By 1984, manufacturing in Britain accounted for less than 25 per cent of the nation's economic activity.

The crisis of the recent recession is only the culmination of decades of decline which have caused Britain to slip from the position of economic preeminence in Europe that it held not so long ago. At the outset of the 1950s, the British were the continent's most prosperous people, barring special cases such as the Swiss and the Swedes who had remained neutral during the Second World War. But France drew level with Britain in the course of the decade and raced ahead after 1960. In the early 1960s, the Germans and the Danes also overtook Britain. For the next 10 years the British economy grew faster than ever before; but it was a

boom time throughout all of Europe, and other economies were growing even more rapidly. The British were outstripped by the Dutch and the Belgians, and the Italians, previously a long way behind, significantly narrowed the gap between economies. By 1980, gross domestic product per head (the nation's output divided by its population) stood at $9,340 in Britain. This remained higher than in Italy, where the backward south kept the equivalent figure down to $6,910, but well behind Germany at $13,310 and France at $12,140.

The story of outpaced growth is repeated in the export figures. In 1958, the United Kingdom accounted for just under one fifth of all the world's manufactured exports; only the United States exported more. By 1981, Britain had slipped to fifth position in the world, behind Germany, the United States, Japan and France, and less than one tenth of goods manufactured in Britain left her ports.

Rightly or wrongly, the pessimists have had the best of the argument within Britain; a majority of commentators, politicians and industrialists have preferred to concentrate on the collapsing manufacturing sector and Britain's relative decline in the international economic league tables relative to its industrial competitors. The danger is that by opting for this gloomy view of the economy, they obscure an equally crucial fact: that the vast majority of

5

Britain's population are far more prosperous than ever before.

This partial blindness has causes deep in history. Britain still has an image of itself, despite the evidence, as one of the world leaders in industry, because it was first in the field: it was where the Industrial Revolution began. And the nation concentrates its attention on manufacturing industry because it was on manufacturing that Britain's industrial might was founded.

The Industrial Revolution took place first in Britain for a variety of reasons—cultural, political, economic and scientific—combined with a certain amount of good luck. British inventors created the machines that made mass production possible and, from about 1750 on, British entrepreneurs willingly moved in to exploit their ideas, while landowners developed mines and transport. Improvements in agriculture freed large numbers of people from the land to work in the factories; a prosperous and expanding population bought the factories' new products; and the government refrained from interfering in events. The net result was that between 1780 and 1800 industrial production doubled—albeit from a very low base—and it went on to multiply a further 14-fold in the next 100 years.

The textile industry was in the vanguard. Newly invented machines for spinning yarn and for weaving cloth were harnessed to steam power, so that vast factories could produce cheaply what had until then been the expensive product of a cottage industry. Manchester in the north-west of England became the centre for spinning, and though much has been made of the damp local climate which made the yarn less likely to snap, two other factors were equally responsible for Manchester's new status. One was the proximity of Liverpool, a major port with traditional links with the United States, the source of most of the raw cotton. The other was the willingness of the local labour force to desert the unrewarding farms on the nearby Pen-

Factory smoke almost obscures the
golden sun rising over the Humber
estuary in north-east England.
Humberside's traditional industry,
steel production, is in decline, but
recently the region has attracted new
oil refineries and chemical plants.

nine range for the challenge of city life.

Manchester also saw the construction of the country's first canal. The Duke of Bridgewater had coal mines on his estates just outside Manchester, and he wished to link them with the heart of the city. In an age when roads were little better than mud tracks, he realized that water was a cheap and effective alternative to packhorses. A huge work force was needed to dig the canal. Thousands of labourers were brought in, many of them from Ireland. But in 1761, when the canal was completed, it cut the cost of delivered coal to just a tenth of its earlier price and rapidly recouped the investment.

The years from 1770 to 1830 saw an amazing boom in canal construction, which gave Britain an unparalleled network of internal communications. This infrastructure speeded up industrial life. It allowed cotton bales from America and wool from Australia to be brought to the heart of the country, where an emerging industrial proletariat turned them into finished goods to be re-exported to a far-flung Empire. Likewise iron ore could be shipped to the newly invented blast furnaces, which spewed out finished sheet metal to be worked into machines and later into the iron ships that carried the expanding trade. And the canals allowed the free movement of coal, the cheap and plentiful fuel which created the steam to power the machines.

Ironically, though it was crucial to the process of industrialization, the canal boom was short-lived. As early as 1825, a railway train ran the 15 kilometres from Darlington to Stockton carrying 450 passengers, and by 1840 the rail network had been developed to a point where it became the canals' deadly rival. The railways surpassed

even the canals in the pace of their development, their stunning feats of engineering—and their spectacular bankruptcies. They created a massive demand for iron rails, thus boosting the iron and steel industry and giving Britain the capacity, once its own boom was over, to supply the rails which opened up the new worlds of North and South America.

Britain's surge of business and economic power, between 1750 and 1914, coincided with the pinnacle of its political power. Each reinforced the other. The growing Empire and the other newly settled lands overseas provided raw materials for Britain's factories and markets for its finished goods. Trade routes were protected by the world's most powerful navy. Of the nation's potential competitors, Germany was not unified until 1871, France was weak and unstable in the aftermath of the Napoleonic wars of the early 19th

century, and the United States was still in the process of developing its vast resources. So Britain was unrivalled, and its dominance came to be associated in the public mind with the mighty staple industries—steel, shipbuilding, coal and textiles.

Britain's early success held the seeds of its subsequent troubles. Manufacturing for the Empire and for other developing territories was fine up to a point, but it did mean that British manufacturers became used to telling their customers what they should have, rather than finding out what was really wanted. Moreover, most of the countries that bought British goods had relatively simple requirements. To meet their needs, Britain kept on making the same basic products while Germany and the United States were gearing themselves up for the production of more sophisticated goods. By 1900, the German chemical industry

A stretch of upland in Wiltshire comes
under the plough in preparation for
barley sowing. Most of the English
farmland is crisscrossed by hedges, but
to accommodate modern, large
agricultural machinery, parts of the
country have been turned into prairie.

117

RELICS OF THE INDUSTRIAL REVOLUTION

The tide of the Industrial Revolution changed the face of Britain for ever as it spread across the country in the 18th and 19th centuries. Rural enclaves disappeared and in their place mushroomed factories and mills, blast furnaces and engine houses, docks and canals. Many of these structures have vanished in their turn under the continued advance of technology, but others still survive in locations as various as the buildings themselves and a few, indeed, are still active.

Among the most poignant relics are the ruins of bygone mining industries set in the heart of the countryside. On the Cornish coast, crumbling stone buildings recall the days when tin and copper were extracted from rich seams in the rock beneath. In Derbyshire, South Wales and the Isle of Man, spectacular remains of once-active lead mines are still to be found.

In the earliest days of automation, factories too were sited amid moors and fields. Running water was the first form of power to be harnessed for mass production, and 18th-century spinning mills were built in upland valleys where tumbling streams could turn their wheels night and day. Later, when coal was used to generate steam power, factories moved into the cities. Today, in many towns of Lancashire and Yorkshire, the gaunt profiles of textile mills evoke busy scenes from the past. And further south, in Staffordshire, the bottle-shaped kilns of pottery works are a distinctive feature of several communities, their domed roofs designed to reflect the heat of the furnace and bake the ceramics evenly.

Deplored when the fumes from their chimneys blighted the surrounding town, the kilns are now carefully preserved. And a similar fate has met other buildings of their epoch. Admired for their power to evoke a pioneering age, they are recognized too as landmarks in their own right, with an idiosyncratic and haunting beauty.

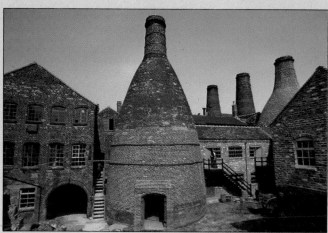
Founded in 1787, this Staffordshire pottery is now a museum.

Abandoned warehouses fringe

At Hebden Bridge in West Yorkshire, trees surround a cotton mill and the workers' housing.

London's Thames.

A cotton mill overlooks a Lancashire canal.

SIR RICHARD ARKWRIGHT & CO.

ESTABLISHED 1769

Yarn is still processed in this 18th-century Derbyshire mill.

An engine-house marks the site of a 19th-century Cornish tin mine.

and the American car industry were much further advanced than their British equivalents. Once the rest of the world began to industrialize, laggardly Britain was very vulnerable.

Then, just when adjustment away from the country's original industrial character might have taken place—in the period between 1914 and 1945—Britain's participation in two world wars further distorted the economy. The prime needs of a military machine are steel, coal, ships—all the heavy industries which should ideally have been run down in favour of more advanced technologies such as chemicals and electrical goods. Instead they were expanded and developed as part of the nation's fight for survival.

Today, though the Empire is gone, Britain still finds it difficult to allow these industries to fade away as they come under threat from more modern and efficient producers in the developing nations. The British have poured in massive subsidies over many years to keep unviable businesses in being, and thereby created a rigid, indeed brittle manufacturing base. It is the collapse of this sector which has caused so much heartsearching and uncertainty in the Britain of the 1980s.

Although today's problems have their roots in history, history cannot be blamed for everything that goes wrong. Governments are appointed to change the course of history, and successive British post-war governments have failed to reverse the downward trend. For all their efforts, they seem rather to have accelerated it.

Since World War II, the state has come to play a prominent part in the British economy. The state owns the basic utilities—electricity, coal, steel,

5

gas, shipbuilding, the railways and the postal services—most of which were nationalized by the Labour government that was in power for six years after World War II. Health care is paid for by the state and free to all, though there are some independent hospitals, clinics and private health insurance schemes. And although well over half of the country's houses are owner-occupied, nearly one third of the housing stock was built and is still owned by local government authorities, who remain by far the largest source of rented accommodation in the country.

The expansion of the state into most corners of national life has meant sharp increases in public spending. In 1959, government spending accounted for 33 per cent of the gross domestic product; by 1974, the figure was 44 per cent. It has never since come down below 40 per cent. In the United States and Japan, government spending is around 30 per cent of the gross domestic product. In France and Germany, as in Britain, the figure is above 40 per cent, but those two countries, being richer than Britain, are better able to support high government spending.

To many in Britain, the heavy involvement of the state in the economy accounts for the nation's poor post-war performance. In a series of articles published in the *Sunday Times* in 1974, two economists, Albert Bacon and Walter Eltis, argued that the growing demands the state was making on the nation's resources were crowding out manufacturing industry and reducing the amount of money available for private spending. Other authorities differ, saying that companies maintained constant investment and profit levels as government spending went up, and they argue instead that, had the public

sector not grown, the wave of mass unemployment that struck in the late 1970s would have hit Britain much sooner than it did.

Even if the level of government involvement in the economy is about right, there remains the question of whether the government is directing the funds at its disposal wisely. Money spent on researching and developing new products is vital to the future of any economy. British spending on both research and development compares favourably with that of most other countries but, often for political reasons, a large part of the resources are diverted into relatively unproductive ends. And inevitably the country's limited stock of innovative and scientific talent is also tied up on those projects.

The best example of such a venture is Concorde, the high-speed passenger aircraft. Research in Britain in the 1950s proved that it was technically possible to build a supersonic commercial carrier. The research also showed that such an aircraft would guzzle so much fuel and would carry so few passengers that nobody was likely to buy it. But the government of the early 1960s, anxious to prevent Britain from slipping in the international technology race, was ready to pursue its goal almost regardless of commercial considerations. With the French as partners, the British went ahead to develop the aeroplane. The initial arrangement was that the development costs would be borne equally by the government and by the aircraft manufacturers. Later, the manufacturers, seeing how unviable the project was, declined to pay their share, and the government picked up the whole cost. Concorde, indisputably a technical marvel and a beautiful object, today makes its super-

sonic transcontinental journeys and provides a profit for British Airways; but the entire research and development costs of more than £1,000 million have had to be written off, and there has not been a single true commercial sale to a foreign airline.

For France, too, the Concorde venture was a disaster, but one from which the French at least learnt some useful lessons about how they should tackle international projects and how to limit government's role in them. In 1970 a new six-nation European aircraft-building consortium, Airbus Industrie, was set up; France was the dominant partner. Run with minimal government interference, Airbus Industrie has been very successful. But when it was floated, Britain, still absorbed with Concorde, secured only a minority stake, although the British aviation industry at the time was technically more advanced than that of France.

Another large slice of Britain's research and development goes on defence. Once again, government projects are conducted at the expense of conventional industry: an electronics company commissioned by the government to do work on armaments such as torpedoes will shift people and resources from development of, say, video recorders. Commercial applications of most defence research are very limited.

The public sector's huge appetite for research and development is thus a cause for concern, but perhaps a less serious one than the government's scope for mismanaging Britain's most basic industries. A number of the industries owned by the state—the mines, the steelworks and the shipyards—are the very ones which needed radically reshaping and contracting

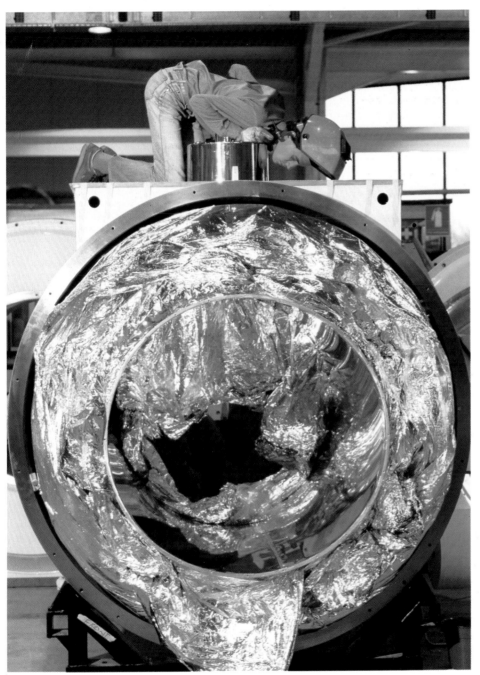

A worker assembles a magnet system that will form the heart of an advanced medical body scanner, able to detect lesions such as tumours in soft tissue. The powerful magnet functions at −269°C; to maintain that temperature, it is enclosed within cooling vessels and layers of insulation.

after World War II. But successive governments have been too close to the problem to grasp it, and all too easily persuaded to prop up the old at the expense of the new. In regions such as the north-east of England, heavy industry provides virtually all the local jobs, and governments have shied from the political consequences of creating pockets of massive unemployment. Even the more modern industries owned by the state have not prospered: again and again, wrong investment decisions have been made, too rigidly adhered to for a while, and then compounded by hasty switches.

All these failings are apparent in the story of the post-war British electrical supply industry. Some key investment errors were made in the 1950s, a period when that industry accounted for one twelfth of all domestic investment. First, engineers installed uneconomically small 30 megawatt and 60 megawatt generator sets with high capital costs and low thermal efficiency. In the late 1950s, that choice was recognized to be short-sighted, and favour fell instead exclusively upon an untried and technically demanding new 500 megawatt design. When the 500 megawatt generators were built, they frequently broke down.

The electricity industry made a second major error in its choice of fuel. Largely because the mines had just been nationalized and the government was heavily committed to coal, British power stations in the 1950s were almost all coal-fired. But coal was expensive and supplies were prone to disruption—partly because many of the seams were in geologically difficult areas but partly too because of recurring industrial disputes. So the nation swung abruptly to nuclear power, not-

5

withstanding its still untested technology. By the early 1960s, more than half the world's nuclear-powered electricity was generated in Britain.

In the following decade, when the rest of Europe's growth was being fuelled by unprecedentedly cheap and plentiful oil, Britain's growth was stunted by expensive energy derived from coal and nuclear fuel. Britain's economy grew during the 1960s at around 3 per cent compared with its rivals' 5 to 6 per cent, and a number of British economists believe that something like a third of the difference in growth rate can be attributed to Britain's high fuel costs.

Determined to boost competition and efficiency in British industry, the Conservative government that came to power in 1979 proposed to play a less direct part in industry and to sell off large chunks of the public sector— among them British Airways and British Telecommunications—to the private sector. Although the decision was probably sound, it illustrates one of the worst traits of recent Britih governments: their inability to create a stable environment in which business can flourish. France, Germany and the United States can change the political complexion of their government without anyone feeling the need to undo all that has been done before. But in Britain, where the political parties hold widely different attitudes to industry, violent about-turns have become all too common. The most extreme case is the steel industry, which was nationalized in 1951, denationalized in 1953 and nationalized once more in 1967. Such reversals can make nonsense of long-term plans developed by businesses. And all too often they serve as an excuse for businessmen not to make long-term plans at all; as a result, they miss those opportunities that do exist.

Trade unions provide another political distraction for businessmen. Britain was one of the first countries to develop trade unions, and one of the first to grant them legal immunity in pursuing an industrial claim. Until the outbreak of the Second World War, union membership was concentrated in the oldest industries, but afterwards it quickly spread to newer industries such as electronics and then to white-collar workers and the professions—teaching, banking, the civil service and so on. Union membership reached a peak in 1979 at 55 per cent of employees; it sank to 50 per cent by the mid-1980s, but membership remained much higher than West Germany's 33 per cent and the United States' 20 per cent.

British trade unions have a great deal of power, for good or ill. In many industries, employees feel a stronger identity with their union than with their company, and many workers who have aspirations to leadership channel their energies more naturally into union work than into management. In some of the industries, it has long been accepted practice for trade-union shop stewards rather than management to take responsibility for the day-to-day decisions on how plants should be run. The shop stewards' first concern is naturally to maximize earnings for their union members.

Most British trade unions represent only people with a particular set of skills; the industry-wide unions found in Germany, for example, are uncommon. Because several rival unions are often active in the same factory, disputes frequently break out over the relative pay of the various groups of workers and over who does what job.

While strife is endemic between the various workers' factions, trust between workers and management is also in short supply and confrontations are frequent. In the 1960s, Britain acquired a reputation for bad industrial relations and damaging strikes. The statistics do not apparently bear this out: between 1964 and 1968, industrial disputes cost Britain an average of 230 days per 1,000 people employed and four countries—Canada, Ireland, Italy and the United States—lost more than four times that amount. But in Britain there were also many niggling, unofficial stoppages, which went unrecorded in the statistics and which reduced the reliability of British suppliers.

In the 1970s, attempts were made to repair past mistakes, and the chosen means was participation. Government led the way in fostering discussions between ministers, representatives of industry and union leaders. Some informal agreements on wage and price restraints were reached, but benefits were temporary, and the feeling of the 1980s was that excess of consultation may have slowed the pace of change.

The event that did make a difference was the recession of the early 1980s, which threw many people out of work and put the initiative back with management. British managers began to display more dynamic leadership than they had for years, and wrested many areas of decision-making back from shop stewards. New legislation curtailed the unions' legal immunities. But it will be some time before British industries have compensated for all the bad practices of the past.

Bad decisions by government account for some of the failures of post-war Bri-

At the Miners' Gala in the northern city of Durham, coal workers and their families parade through the streets. Held every year since 1871, the event combines political speeches with entertainment—picnics, brass band recitals and fairground festivities.

tish industry, bad labour relations for others. But a number of historians believe that these two factors have a common root: a disdain for industry that pervades British life. And while it would be rash to make too much of something so intangible, there is some evidence to suggest that the British really are more antagonistic to industry than most other nations.

One indication is the failure of the British to make commercial use of their scientific discoveries. The British have an exceptional record in science and invention. Since 1901, when the Nobel prizes were first awarded, the British have won 17 per cent of the prizes for physics, chemistry and medicine—a higher proportion than any other nation except the U.S. Britons invented jet engines, hovercraft and linear motors for high-speed urban transport; in the mid-20th century, they played a crucial part in the development of computers. Yet none of these breakthroughs was wholeheartedly followed up in Britain. Other nations developed them to commercial usefulness.

A second gauge of British attitudes to industry comes from surveys of workers and their motivation, which consistently reveal a lack of interest in profit, whether it be individual or corporate. A recent poll, for example, found that 51 per cent of responders would not work longer even if it meant earning more money, and 56 per cent had no personal drive to be rich. Another part of the same poll suggested that the satisfaction most people got from work came from the pleasures of companionship and of doing an interesting job.

Another poll put an interesting twist on this finding. Contradicting the persistent myth that the British are a workshy nation, it showed that of all the peoples in Europe, the British took by far the most pride in their work. Seventy-nine per cent took a "great deal of pride" against only 13 per cent of French and 15 per cent of Germans. And while 17 per cent of French admitted to taking no pride in their work at

all, only 1 per cent of Britons would make such an admission. This finding ties in with a criticism that has long been levelled against British manufactures—that while they are often poorly designed, they are excessively well-made, built to last 100 years even when the need was for a product that would last for only 10.

The ambivalence about industry revealed by British attitudes to scientific innovation and to their own work is something that goes back a long way. The British were not only the inventors of industrial life, they were also the first to turn against it. Already in the 19th century, influential writers such as John Ruskin and Charles Dickens were condemning the pursuit of wealth and the brutality and ugliness that seemed inseparable from the so-called progress of their age. Dickens' campaign against the dehumanizing effects of industry culminated in his novel of 1854, *Hard Times*, which portrayed the grimness of a fictional Coketown—a place modelled on the new industrial cities in the north of England.

Many historians attribute the persistence of these anti-industrial sentiments to Britain's class system. The tendency of workers to place their trade unions higher in their loyalties than their employers, for example, reflects their traditional class solidarity. Meanwhile the British middle classes, still a little in love with the aristocracy, deeply admire the things the aristocrats hold dear—a leisurely pace of life, the peace of the countryside, and the maintenance of things as they always have been. Industry does not sit comfortably with such values. In the public schools, where the children of the middle class are sent to become gentlemen, generations of pupils have been imbued with an antipathy to industry.

Today, public schools pride themselves on their science teaching, and a generation is growing up with few of the traditional prejudices. But the change of emphasis is not many years old, and the majority of those who hold high positions in government, the civil

124

The Bank of England *(left)* and its high-rise neighbour, the Stock Exchange *(centre background)*, stand at the hub of the commercial area known as the City of London. The City is one of the world's leading markets for shares, gold, shipping and insurance.

service, finance and the professions have been through an education system that discouraged them from taking industry seriously. With Britain's ruling élite so out of sympathy with industry, it becomes clearer why recent British governments have done the economy more harm than good.

Meanwhile, good engineers are thin on the ground because of the low status and low salary they command, and those that exist rarely rise high up the corporate ladder. Typically, these engineers lose out to professional men—accountants and lawyers. Their low standing helps to explain why it is that business has been tardy in exploiting British inventions.

So it is partly through the choice of the British people, who have refused to let the values of industry dominate their thinking, that Britain has lost its 50-year lead over other nations. Yet the British temperament is not at odds with all economic endeavour. Heavy industry excites the strongest antipathy; other forms of money-making, such as commerce, are perfectly acceptable. Britain's saving economic strength has long been its service industries.

The City, with its myriad financial institutions, is the best showcase for the nation's skills in the service sector. But British distribution and retailing are also impressive. The national newspapers, for example, which are printed each night in London, rely on superb timing and an extensive railway network to whisk them by morning to the farthest corners of the country. A remarkable nationwide rental network has long supplied nearly half of the nation's televisions, and in the early 1980s it branched out into video recorders. At a time when technology was developing so fast that buying video recorders was a risky and expensive proposition, the rental facilities meant that Britain was the fastest-growing market in the world for video.

Chain stores such as Marks and Spencer offer customers consistently high quality and value, partly thanks to a highly efficient stock control which in turn depends on a reliable and regular delivery of replacement goods. The absence of any similarly efficient backup in other countries of Europe is one reason why British retail chains have found it difficult to establish their presence abroad.

It is no coincidence that some of the most successful entrepreneurs in Britain since the Second World War have been retailers. Sir Terence Conran, the founder of the furniture store Habitat, epitomizes them. Born in 1931 to middle-class parents, Conran was sent to a minor public school, Bryanston, which was liberal enough to teach him welding and metalwork. He went on to the Central School of Arts and Crafts in London and began to design furniture. Next came a spell of flat-sharing with the sculptor Eduardo Paolozzi, who taught him to appreciate objects in three dimensions and—just as useful—good cooking.

Conran wanted to make furniture, but he needed cash. So in the early 1950s he started a restaurant, then opened two more. He sold the lot, opened a fourth restaurant and sold out again. Two years of hard work and fast deals left him £6,000 to the good, and with that he launched his furniture business. The early days were tough—and made tougher, Conran concluded, by the inability of the existing furniture stores to sell his goods effectively. So, in desperation, in 1964 he opened his first store in London's Fulham Road—as much to show lacklustre retailers how his furniture should be presented and sold as from a desire to become a retailer in his own right.

His concept for the store was to have one model of every single item a young couple would need to furnish a home. The things had to be well made, well designed to appeal to the fashion-conscious, and reasonably priced. The formula worked so well that Conran soon established himself as designer to a whole British generation, and he eventually expanded successfully into Europe and the United States. In the late 1970s, Conran's group went public, making him a multimillionaire, and in the 1980s he started expanding anew: he bought the Mothercare chain—a one-time success, selling maternity and baby wear, which had failed to adjust to the end of the baby

A member of the Metal Exchange in London makes his bid for a consignment of Peruvian copper. Like the other great trading institutions of the City, the Metal Exchange links buyers and sellers worldwide.

INSIGNIA OF ANCIENT TRADES

The arms of the Haberdashers.

The arms of the Fishmongers.

The arms of the Ironmongers.

The arms of the Merchant Tailors.

Amid the bustle of the modern City of London, ancient trade guilds continue to flourish. Also known as livery companies because of the distinctive dress their members used to wear, these archaic institutions lend colour and flamboyance to life in the City.

Deriving from Saxon associations of merchants and craftsmen, the guilds rose to eminence in the Middle Ages and came to dominate the commercial and political life of the City. Some 90 of the guilds survive, most in possession of fine premises, a precious collection of silver, a coat of arms bearing the symbols of their calling *(above)* and a tradition of lavish entertainment. It is rare now for a guild to have more than a nominal connection with its old trade—the Goldsmiths, Vintners and Fishmongers are exceptions—and most exist simply as social and charitable organizations, with members drawn from every trade and profession. Membership is usually passed from father to son, but distinguished outsiders are sometimes invited to join.

boom of the early 1970s—and then proceeded to revamp it; he also became involved in fashion retailing.

Conran's quick wits and innovative selling methods illustrate one set of the British service sector's strengths. On the surface, the City seems to represent very different virtues, because its most obvious feature is stability. But the City too has repeatedly shown itself able to move with the times in order to keep its premier position in world financial markets.

The City acquired its importance soon after Britain industrialized. Because a large proportion of Britain's output went overseas, there was an early need for the complex arrangements that sustain international trade. By the 1870s, the whole panoply of modern financial services had evolved.

International banks provided finance in the farthest corners of the globe. Lloyds emerged as the first and still the world's foremost insurance market, a place where it is possible to insure absolutely anything, provided the client is prepared to pay the premium. The Baltic Exchange became the centre for placing cargoes on the world's merchant fleets. The profession of accountancy developed in the City, which also housed the world's first commodity markets, where cocoa and coffee, rubber and wool could be traded. Later came metal markets for tin, lead and copper, and the bullion market, for many years the world centre for gold dealing, which even today shares the honours with Zurich and New York. The Stock Exchange developed in time to finance much of the expansion of British industry and to raise considerable sums for development overseas.

The City grew and prospered, helped by the political stability of the

The City of London has its own "Parliament", the Court of Common Council, which meets in the medieval Guildhall (above). The council is elected by local residents, but its leader, the Lord Mayor, is chosen by the City's trade guilds.

5

Victorian age and by Britain's freedom from exchange controls in the 19th century. Sterling became a reserve currency, used, like gold, to finance deals between any two countries so as to avoid arguments about exchange rates. The custodian of standards for all of these financial deals was the Bank of England—the central bank of the United Kingdom, which issues notes and acts as banker to the government and to other banks.

The Bank of England has always been prepared to intervene to ensure the system's economic stability. In 1890, for example, Barings, one of the oldest of London's merchant banks, overreached itself on a loan to Argentina; the Argentine economy collapsed, threatening to take its creditor with it, but the Bank of England salvaged the house rather than risk the ruin of the whole system.

Today, the City remains pre-eminent, despite the efforts of New York and Zurich to mount a challenge. One reason for its continued success is that, unlike the American financial sector, it is comparatively free from regulation. It sometimes takes American bankers and financiers months of negotiation to obtain permission for new activities which in London is granted in a few minutes. In the City, the only real authority is that of the Bank of England which, although nationalized since 1946, sees itself as quite independent of the government. The Bank will signify its approval or disapproval of a deal or a form of business conduct, and a hint of displeasure is normally enough to bring erring banks or stockbrokers back into line.

But in the early 1970s, the Bank of England let its guard slip. It had allowed a rapid expansion of "fringe"

banks: small concerns lending largely for speculative property development. The Bank failed to ensure that their policies were as prudent as those of the long-established high-street organizations. When the property boom gradually levelled off, one bank collapsed and others followed it down in a chain reaction. With hindsight the crisis looked inevitable, but it still shook the City to its foundations. In the aftermath, the Bank of England was seen at its best: it organized a rescue, forcing strong institutions to take on the debts of the weak to prevent the collapse of the system as a whole.

The early 1980s have seen the Bank as innovator, acting to bring about the reform of the stock market. The City, although so impressive in its entirety, has traditionally been made up of a multiplicity of small, undercapitalized financial institutions. Much larger units are the norm in the United States and Japan. Senior officials in the Bank and government became concerned that, as telecommunications turned the world into a single global market place, London would lose its business to the foreign giants.

The Bank of England's solution has been to encourage the formation of conglomerates which combine the skills of stockbroking, banking, insurance and corporate finance supplied by different firms. The new, heavyweight financial institutions that are emerging have the resources to open up foreign branches and let some of them operate at a loss, and to invest in new technology; they seem well able to meet the challenge of the international arena.

While the City has sometimes seemed almost the only bright spot in the British economy, it has in two senses enjoyed its success at the expense of the rest of the economy. In the first place, the City's special needs have damaged other industries financially. Because sterling was in the past used to transact so much international trade, the government often felt the need to stabilize its value so that overseas holders of British currency did not suffer a capital loss. So if interest rates in London were less attractive than the rates in New York, tempting overseas banks and businesses with deposits in pounds to convert them into dollars and thus push down the exchange rate, the Bank of England often increased interest rates to attract the deposits back. But these higher interest rates hit industry: they obliged companies to defer or cancel new investments because they could no longer afford to borrow.

Since 1972, when sterling was allowed to float without too much government interference, this problem has been less acute. But the city still inflicts another blight on industry, by snatching up more than its share of the ambitious and gifted. Financial rewards for those who succeed either in banking or the Stock Exchange are considerably higher than would be achieved by a similar high-flier employed in industry, and London has more appeal as a place to live in than the industrial cities of the Midlands and the north of England.

Yet in spite of these and other difficulties, the British economy gives cause for optimism. The companies that have survived the recession of the early 1980s are as efficient and productive as most of the international competition. The British car industry, for example, has improved the productivity of its workers and the reliability of its products and stemmed the tide of imports which in the late 1970s threatened to overwhelm it. The direction in which industry worldwide is evolving is one that suits British talents. And revenues from North Sea oil fields have bought more time in which industry can adjust to the new trends.

It is unrealistic to think of Britain competing as a manufacturer with the established giants, the United States and Japan. But it is not at all impossible for Britain to hold its own in the new technologies—in the development and application of software for the forthcoming generations of computers, in biotechnology and in advanced engineering such as satellite manufacture. All these areas rely far less on the ability to organize and discipline hundreds of employees than on the skills and lateral thinking of a few gifted individuals. The success of the City relies on just such cerebral skills. The British enthusiasm for computers suggests that they can turn these skills to new uses. Moreover, as industry comes increasingly to resemble the professions, it seems certain that the anti-industrial mood that has long hung over Britain will lift.

The question for the 1980s is whether the necessary changes can be brought about quickly enough. At present, North Sea oil provides a crucial 6 per cent of the government's tax revenues. Without North Sea oil, taxes on individuals would be so high as to send the British economy into deep depression. Although the oil will last well into the next century, the flow will start to ease off after 1990. The future of Britain therefore hinges on whether enough new enterprises are started in the 1980s, while the going is still good, to ensure the growth of the economy when the oil starts to dry up.

Behind the dome of a 19th-century bank in the City of London, a glass-fronted skyscraper reflects an office block under construction. New and old are juxtaposed everywhere in the City, which was founded by the Romans but radically rebuilt several times.

THE ARDUOUS LIFE OF THE OFFSHORE OILMEN

Photographs by Michael St. Maur Sheil

Britain's North Sea oilfields are a vital new source of wealth, but the treasure lies under stormy seas up to 200 metres deep, trapped at a pressure of some 415 kilograms per square centimetre beneath a sea floor of solid rock up to 3,500 metres thick. To perform the momentous task of getting the oil ashore, hundreds of men live on the lonely production platforms that dot the British sector of the fields. For intensive two-week periods of almost unrelieved work, their lives are bounded by the dark skies and heaving swell of one of the world's most hostile seas; then they are airlifted out for a fortnight of hard-earned recovery, while another tested crew takes their place.

The Brent field, where these pictures were taken, is one of the largest of the developments and one of the most northerly. From its four colossal platforms, grouped 200 kilometres from the Scottish mainland, 176 kilometres of sea-bed pipeline take the oil to the Shetland terminal of Sullom Voe. Each platform, accommodating some 120 men, is as cramped yet as efficiently self-contained as a battleship. On its area of around 4,000 square metres is stacked massive and sophisticated equipment—for drilling and pumping the oil, for repair and maintenance, and for the care of the crews—that would cover a 40,000-square-metre site on land.

The complex activities of the men on the platform are planned to dovetail with the same efficiency as the plant itself. While the "roughnecks"—the team who do the tough and dirty work of drilling—are wrestling with cumbersome equipment, engineers and computer operators are constantly monitoring and adjusting the flow of oil; support services of every kind are provided by the men who drive the cranes, operate the radios, cook the meals and nurse the casualties. As each shift goes off duty, other men instantly take over. For an oil platform never sleeps: it must be in constant production to justify the huge investment sunk in it.

Flares of waste gas brighten the dusk around three oil production platforms in the Brent field. Linked to one of them *(left)* by a gangplank that is removed in rough weather is a semi-submersible vessel—a floating rig used for extra accommodation and as a hospital ship.

130

ANATOMY OF A PRODUCTION PLATFORM

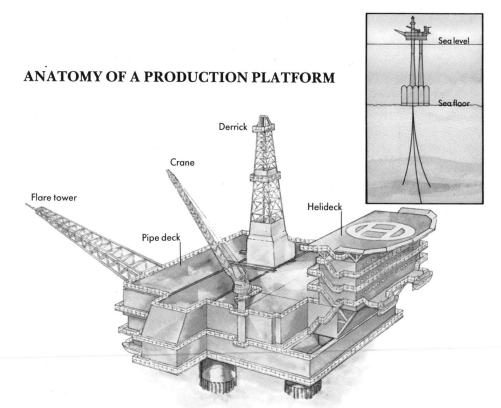

Derrick

Crane

Flare tower

Pipe deck

Helideck

Sea level

Sea floor

Only a fraction of the 300-metre height of a North Sea oil production platform is visible above the surface of the sea *(inset, left)*. The steel or concrete legs that make up two thirds of its size are ballasted down to rest on the sea bed. The superstructure, known as the topsides, includes living quarters, a helicopter landing deck and a flare tower where gas is burnt off; the conspicuous steel derrick and the pipe deck are given over to the business of drilling into the bedrock.

Drilling a single well can take many months. The drill crew extend a conductor pipe to the sea bed from any one of 40 or so slots in the pipe deck. The drilling bit and collar with attached sections of drill pipe are lowered through the conductor pipe. As the drill bores into the rock, more sections of pipe are added. Every so often, the drill bit blunts; to change it, the men must pull up the whole column of pipe, uncouple each joint and stack the sections in the derrick.

When the drill eventually breaks through into the reservoir, the oil rises under its own pressure through the conductor pipe. As the pressure drops, water or gas must be pumped down through other pipes to maintain it and keep the oil flowing.

Men working at a well hole are spattered with "drilling mud"—a substance used to lubricate the drilling bit in action and flush away rock cuttings.

From his perch high in the derrick, a
worker wearing a safety harness awaits
a signal from the well head far below.
The derrick man's job is to shackle
stored lengths of drill pipe as they are
needed to the claw of the pulley that
will swing them down to the well head.

In the pump room, two maintenance engineers check the equipment that will transport the oil on its long journey to the shore. The pipe in the foreground joins on to the major sea-bed pipeline that will conduct the oil to Britain's largest oil terminal, in the Shetland Islands.

A bank of visual display screens gives information on the temperature, flow and pressure of oil to the technicians in the platform's control room. Each platform has its own control system, which transmits data simultaneously to the control room and to the operations headquarters in Aberdeen.

Supply-boat crewmen attach cables to pipeline sections that will be hoisted aboard the platform by crane. All supplies must be brought by boat.

An off-duty worker reads and listens to music in his shared cabin. Most platforms also provide a gymnasium, a games room and a lounge, but the 12-hour shifts are too arduous to leave the men with enough energy for strenuous leisure-time pursuits.

At the end of a shift, men eat in the self-service restaurant. Only soft drinks are served; the complex machinery of a production platform, combined with the often extreme weather conditions, makes it a potentially hazardous place, and the drinking of alcohol is banned for both safety and social reasons.

At the end of their spell on the platform, the men hurry towards the helicopter that will fly them to Aberdeen. The icy waters of the North Sea can render a man unconscious in minutes, so each man wears an insulated waterproof suit to give him a chance of survival in an emergency.

Protected by umbrellas from a summer shower, two Londoners listen to a regimental band performing in a park. Band music is especially popular in the north of England, where brass ensembles belonging to collieries and factories have long provided a focus for intense local loyalty.

EBULLIENCE IN THE ARTS

Ambivalence and controversy have surrounded the idea of culture in Britain ever since it was first thrust upon the nation by Victorian prophets, such as the historian Thomas Carlyle, the poet Matthew Arnold and the critic John Ruskin. Before the 19th century, Britain did not want for what we would now call culture. But such treasures as the glorious buildings of York and Bath, the language of Chaucer and Shakespeare, the music of Purcell, and the paintings of Hogarth and Gainsborough simply existed within the fabric of everyday life. A telling indication of British attitudes is the way London's St. Paul's Cathedral—the masterpiece of the 17th-century architect Christopher Wren—rises sheer from a warren of offices and small buildings; other nations would have provided such a building with a portentous setting, but none of the plans to surround St. Paul's with a great piazza were ever carried out. Similarly, London's splendid 19th-century Royal Opera House is tucked away near the city's former vegetable market instead of gracing a major thoroughfare.

The Victorian urge to reassess cultural landmarks such as these was inspired by Britain's industrial revolution, and the physical suffering and spiritual starvation it induced. Perhaps, the new thinking went, examples of the high achievements of which humanity was capable would relieve the grimness men saw around them. It was an idea borrowed from Germany, where culture had long been considered superior to everyday life, and

represented ideals towards which all right-thinking people aspired.

Arnold was the first Englishman to write of culture in this sense. And he added a second word to the English language when he accused the wealthy new manufacturing classes of a crime not previously recorded on the moral statute book of the United Kingdom.

"Philistinism!" he thundered. "We have not the expression in English. Maybe we have not the word because we have so much of the thing." The antidote to the force called philistinism was the counter-force called culture, which Arnold bravely defined as "acquainting ourselves with the best that has been known and said in the world. . . Culture looks beyond machinery, culture hates hatred; culture has one great passion, the passion for sweetness and light. It has one even yet greater—the passion for making them *prevail.*"

It was a noble shot at the indefinable, and one that inspired, whether they were aware of it or not, providers of 20th-century sweetness and light such as John Reith, first director of the state-financed broadcasting company, the BBC, who recognized and developed the new medium's power to educate and inform; Allen Lane, who founded the Penguin paperback imprint and made hundreds of literary classics available cheaply for the first time; and Robert Mayer, whose Youth and Music organization was still sponsoring orchestral concerts, opera and ballet performances for schoolchildren and young people when he celebrated his hundredth birthday in 1979. Heroes

such as these fought all their lives to define standards and disseminate quality, and their efforts have borne a rich harvest. The arts scene in Britain today is one of the liveliest in the world.

But the slightly bossy note of Arnold's cultural evangelism also helped to give culture a restricted meaning and a dubious name which it has never lost. Most British people still associate culture exclusively with literature, the fine arts and the performing arts—phenomena designed, so the thinking goes, just to amuse the middle classes. Philistinism still flourishes. Arnold's culture is suspect to three powerful and vocal sets of opponents on three separate accounts: to patriots and chauvinists because the concept came from abroad; to egalitarians because it smacks of posh art dispensed from above, like a prize for political good conduct; to patricians because it offers a dangerous key for all men to enter a commonwealth of knowledge and understanding free from the historic confinements of job, money and class.

Slowly, however, the idea is spreading that culture might be a less narrow and less controversial thing—that it might also embrace an entire national heritage of self-expression, social attitudes and behaviour. There is growing acceptance that it includes, for instance, pop music, a field in which contemporary Britain excels; the walking clubs that foster enthusiasm for the British landscape; and even the industrial machinery, now obsolete, which Ruskin and Arnold deplored. The British Council, promoter of Britain's cultural

6

image abroad, interprets its responsibilities in the broadest way. It not only supports tours by British artists, musicians, writers and actors but also, largely by organizing visits to Britain, disseminates such exportable aspects of Britain's heritage as parliamentary democracy, the rule of law, the technology of fishing gear and, most widely popular of all English inventions, football. In short, the Council defines British culture as the British way of life.

Serious analysis of the British way of life is rare, and George Orwell remains one of its shrewdest and most fearless commentators more than 30 years after his death. The visitor to Britain, wrote Orwell towards the end of World War II, would almost certainly find "the salient characteristics of the English common people to be artistic insensibility, gentleness, respect for legality, suspicion of foreigners, sentimentality about animals, hypocrisy, exaggerated class distinctions and an obsession with sport." Each of these points is valid today, to a greater or lesser degree.

The degrees of difference are illuminating. If gentleness and a respect for legality are less in evidence after two decades of post-imperial frustration and the temptations of the black economy, so too is hypocrisy. Class distinctions, though less exaggerated, still exist—shifting this way and that, bewildering outside observers. Suspicion of foreigners and sentimentality towards animals are as firmly rooted as ever—most people have learnt nothing positive or useful about the nation's European neighbours from Britain's membership of the EEC, and cats stuck up chimneys still make the main evening television news. The national obsession with sport has mushroomed with the growth of television to the

An acrobatic fire-eater entertains the idlers in the cobbled piazza of Covent Garden, a fashionable shopping area in London. Buskers must audition for this prime pitch, but elsewhere in London they perform without ceremony wherever they find a good spot.

point where it involves most members of the family—wives and mothers scarcely less than the rest.

The startling change here, which Orwell would certainly have observed, is that by the mid-1980s the fastest-growing sports in Britain, historic home of team spirit and what even the French call *le fairplay*, exalted the gladiatorial contest that leads to individual victory: golf, tennis, athletics, squash, snooker. Humour is never quite absent, however. It is most evident in wrestling, a sport considered by Japan and Britain to be peculiarly their own. While Japanese wrestling is deadly serious, British "all-in" wrestling is a cheerful spectator sport, particularly enjoyed by older working-class women, which deliberately parodies the competitiveness of the male. Before the fight begins, contestants indulge in a display of outrageous vanity, strutting and preening in gorgeous costumes; when they are locked in battle, cheating—or at least a pretence of it—is obligatory.

The one charge of Orwell's which can be seriously questioned today is

that of artistic insensibility. At the time he was writing, Orwell had a case: professional theatre, music and fine art involved only a minority and the mass of the public were indifferent to them. Now, however, the philistines, though still numerous, have only a bare majority. A survey conducted in the early 1980s revealed that in the course of a year 40 per cent of those questioned had been to the opera, theatre, ballet or a concert, and 45 per cent had visited a museum or art gallery.

Orwell, moreover, had failed to take account of a unique ingredient in British cultural life: participation. The British do not wait for art to be brought to them: they create it themselves and always have done. The level of amateur involvement in the arts is probably the highest in the world.

The British, for example, act in amateur theatricals to an extent unknown in continental Europe. They play in brass bands. In their thousands, they write poetry and even novels for pleasure rather than publication. They raise such activities as gardening and pigeon breeding to the status of an art. And they fill amateur choirs.

There are no fewer than 700 choirs affiliated to the National Federation of Music Societies—more choirs perform more works than anywhere. Many grew out of the miserable industrial environments of the 19th-century Midlands, Scotland and northern England. The Welsh male voice choir displays a peculiar resonance, power and talent for triple *pianissimo* that brings tears to the eyes of the least sensitive.

The finest amateur choirs—the Philharmonia Chorus, for example, and the Huddersfield Choral Society—perform regularly with top-class professional orchestras and soloists; the chance to

On the sunlit lawns at Glyndebourne in Sussex, where opera is performed in a country-house setting, family parties devote the long dinner interval to lavish picnics. The once-exclusive productions of the Glyndebourne summer festival nowadays tour the country off season.

build up a working relationship with superb musicians is part of the volunteers' reward. But the most eccentric British choral event is an encounter of a single evening's duration. Once a year since 1974, anyone can come to London's Royal Albert Hall and take part in an impromptu rendering of Handel's oratorio *Messiah* under the baton of a first-rate professional conductor. The "*Messiah* from scratch", as it is now known, is hardly the most sensitive rendering. But for the 4,000 singers, most of them keen participants in conventional choirs, the setting and the sheer volume of noise they produce make it an exhilarating experience.

The British participate unselfconsciously in such activities. They join in for fun, in much the same spirit as they would drop into the pub for a pint of beer. They value their leisure keenly as an antidote to the routines of work, and singing or acting mean one more source of variety, one more set of faces.

They cannot summon quite the same relaxed attitude to professional culture, which remains in a separate compartment of their lives. But for an increasing number of British people, it is a very important compartment indeed. In theatre, music and television, Britain produces some of the best work in the world, and the public's enthusiasm matches the excellence and variety of the cultural offerings.

If the plays of William Shakespeare constituted Britain's total cultural heritage, it would still be an immeasurably rich one. But Shakespeare's contemporaries made no mean contribution to English drama, and each succeeding generation's playwrights and actors in turn have added to Britain's brilliant theatrical tradition. They were always

6

obliged to make their appeal to ordinary people rather than to a royal court, for Britain is unusual among European countries in lacking a long tradition of state patronage of the performing arts. Associating national cultural institutions with the empty gestures of pompous and petty states, the British left the arts to fend for themselves.

As a result of this policy—or lack of it—lyric and dramatic theatre were flourishing in Britain by the turn of the 20th century, but haphazardly. For their Saturday night's entertainment, the working classes flocked to the music halls—originally adjuncts of pubs, but subsequently full-scale theatres—to hear sentimental and sardonic vocal numbers interspersed with comic sketches. The middle-class theatres concentrated on comedies and revues; the private operators who ran them rarely risked putting on Shakespearean tragedy, grand opera or unknown playwrights, and when they did, the performances often left much to be desired.

The theatrical goods on offer depended largely on where the potential

theatre-goer lived. Small towns were poorly catered for. Large provincial cities built their cultural life round vast and poorly appointed buildings designed to take spectacular music hall, pantomime and touring shows from London. In London itself, if the quality was sometimes lacking, there was at least ample choice.

By the latter half of the 20th century, both the quality and quantity of British theatrical offerings had improved astoundingly. State patronage of the performing arts was now firmly established, though it remained a sensitive issue. Operators became more adventurous and audiences continued to broaden both socially and geographically. The change was gradual and many people helped it along, but one name in particular stood out: Lilian Baylis, whose efforts in the first half of the century begat no fewer than three of today's major performing companies.

Lilian Baylis had little formal education, artistic talent or money of her own, but possessed extraordinary courage and determination to provide the beauties of Shakespeare, opera and ballet for a public deprived of all three. Universally known in showbusiness as The Lady, she was the epitome of English eccentricity, pragmatism and self-help. She considered that her chief supporter was God, with whom she was famously direct, vigorously invoking His aid for successful first nights.

It was only by chance that she acquired her mission and the means of realizing it. Her Aunt Emma ran the Royal Victoria Hall in South London's slums for a charitable foundation dedicated to providing "purified entertainment" in a teetotal environment for the working man and his family. In 1898, Lilian Baylis went to work for her aunt,

and for the next 14 years she helped put on variety shows, scientific lectures and opera recitals. In 1912, Aunt Emma died and Lilian Baylis took over the management of the Old Vic, as it became known. She promptly staged full-length opera and Shakespeare, and over the years built up a fanatically loyal audience in the seedy, unfashionable building that she had inherited. All the great actors of the time—John Gielgud, Laurence Olivier and Ralph Richardson among them—learnt part of their craft at the Old Vic, which became the seedbed from which Britain's National Theatre germinated. In 1931, Lilian Baylis expanded into a second theatre, Sadler's Wells in north London, where Britain's first permanent ballet company and its first company for the performance of opera in English were born.

Three years later, equally far-sighted lovers of the arts founded one of the most typically British of all the nation's cultural institutions—the Glyndebourne Festival Opera. It has flourished to this day, funding itself entirely by box office returns and business sponsorship. The site of the festival is a private estate in Sussex; the lawns and flowers that surround the opera house provide an unforgettable ambience for the four-month summer opera season. For more than 50 years, audiences have picnicked in evening dress below the green Sussex Downs during the long interval and walked in the scented dusk after the performance. The idyllic surroundings would make the evening a delight regardless of the singing, and inevitably part of the audience treat Glyndebourne simply as a wonderful social occasion. The majority, though, love opera and know that the performances at Glyndebourne will be very

While the referee of an all-in wrestling bout intervenes to detach one hand from an illegal hold, the gleeful offender screws a further grimace from his opponent with the other. Professional wrestling draws frenzied audiences and a huge television public.

good indeed. Such is the festival's reputation for quality that, although the singers are paid less than in other opera houses, there is no shortage of first-class talent anxious for the privilege of working there.

While Glyndebourne's birth made 1934 special, the inter-war span will be remembered in the British theatre for its great performers. Year after year, the actors nurtured by Lilian Baylis shone in the classics, from Shakespeare to Ibsen and Chekhov, but little new British work of lasting importance was written. Meanwhile, the music hall went into decline as the cinema made inroads into its audiences.

World War II brought about a fundamental change in British attitudes towards arts funding. Entertaining the troops to keep up their morale suddenly became a national priority, and public money was found to provide them with the highest quality available. Out of this ad hoc arrangement grew Britain's first system of state patronage. In 1946, the state committed itself to involvement in the arts in peacetime, and set up the autonomous Arts Council to administer the modest funds that were allocated to them.

The public money came in time to nourish and sustain an astonishing creative flowering. The new vigour was first seen in 1956 with the premiere of John Osborne's *Look Back in Anger*. With unprecedented realism, the play expressed the disorientation and the bitterness of the post-war generation.

Laurence Olivier starred in John Osborne's next play, *The Entertainer*, as the seedy music hall comic Archie Rice, whose tatty act, smutty jokes and pathetic married life offered a metaphor for the state of England itself, always the principal theme of Osborne's work. "Don't clap too hard," Archie would taunt the audience, "it's a very old building." Olivier's successful gamble in accepting a contemporary role made it impossible for Britain's other leading actors to stick exclusively to the classical diet any longer; in the later years of their careers, John Gielgud, Ralph Richardson and such other acting luminaries as Alec Guinness and Paul Scofield extended their range with

143

PERENNIAL DELIGHTS OF CHELSEA'S FLOWER SHOW

When the Royal Horticultural Society's great spring show takes place each May, colour and hubbub fill the grounds of London's 17th-century Royal Chelsea Hospital.

On stands lining the aisles of a 12,000-square-metre marquee, nurserymen from all over the British Isles and beyond mass together hundreds of their proudest blooms, all conjured into flower at the critical moment. Some re-create ambitious natural settings—woodland, heath, seaside, pond and stream—to display their specialities.

On the day before the show opens, the exhibits are judged and members of the Royal Family pay a visit. The first day of the four-day show is reserved for Society members and important guests. Thereafter the public flocks in, cramming the marquee, craning to see the flowers, cross-questioning exhibitors and reviving themselves with lobster and champagne. As the show closes, exhibits are sold to the enthusiasts.

A cheerful crowd heads home from the flower show, burdened with unwieldy spoils sold off at the end of the last day.

At the Chelsea Flower Show, a delphinium fancier photographs new strains *(right)*, **a connoisseur scrutinizes a point of interest through a magnifying glass** *(centre)*, **and a grower responds authoritatively to an enquiring customer** *(bottom)*.

contemporary character roles.

Two years after Osborne's arrival, a 28-year-old actor called Harold Pinter made his writing debut on the London stage with his play *The Birthday Party*. Contemporary audiences rejected it, but his next play, *The Caretaker*, was a long-running success, and his cerebral, introverted works are internationally better known now than Osborne's. Osborne and Pinter were merely the first comets in a renaissance of playwrights who have flourished ever since through many phases and styles—rhetorical, ascetic, Marxist, semantic, absurd, farcical, musical. Perhaps not since Shakespeare's age has Britain produced such a diversity of talent.

In the 1960s the new energy that had first erupted in the theatre spread to all the arts in Britain. The Beatles arrived, placing Britain in the forefront of pop music; and, under the conductor Georg Solti, the Royal Opera House at Covent Garden became an international centre of musical and dramatic excellence, encouraging a whole new generation of young performers. The world was enamoured with British painters, sculptors and designers: Henry Moore with his huge reclining figures in stone or bronze; Francis Bacon and his vision of tortured humanity; the witty and endlessly inventive draughtsman and painter David Hockney; and Mary Quant, the fashion designer who popularized the mini skirt.

The abundance of talent made it easy to justify spending more on the arts, and in turn the money encouraged new talent. Arts Council funding doubled between 1963 and 1967, and since 1967 its budget has again more than doubled in real terms. However, Britain has still not caught up with France and Germany in its overall arts spending.

6

British opera and theatre, in particular, are poorly subsidized in comparison with continental practice, making the level of excellence regularly achieved all the more remarkable.

The largest theatrical companies are the Royal Shakespeare Company and the National Theatre, both products of the 1960s and heavily subsidized by the Arts Council. The RSC plays at Stratford upon Avon and London's Barbican Centre, and tours the provinces. Its best work has extended from the entire Shakespearean canon to a nine-hour adaptation of Dickens' *Nicholas Nickleby* and the Edwardian fantasy *Peter Pan*. The National moved in 1976 from the Old Vic to a purpose-built complex on the South Bank of the Thames. Its scope is even less predictable than the RSC's; at the start of the 1980s it struck gold with both the *Oresteia* of Aeschylus and the musical *Guys and Dolls*.

Besides these two giants, London boasts over 40 commercial theatres and nearly as many again on the fringe. In the provinces, the huge Victorian theatres have either gone over to bingo,

been demolished or, in a few cases, been modernized to house opera and dance companies. New small theatres have been built jointly by the Arts Council and local authorities; a strong local commitment supports them. Both within and outside the capital, flexible freelance groups of independent actors and directors play an increasingly important role. Such troupes come together for a show or two and tour the country, playing in pubs, clubs, disused warehouses or any other available and sympathetic space.

If the 20th century has become something of a golden age for dramatic and lyric theatre in Britain, classical music has been at least as blessed. In the 19th century, the Germans dubbed Britain the "land without music". It was not a fair verdict even then, but today the charge would never be made: London is the largest centre for Western classical music-making in the world.

Edward Elgar (1857–1934) was the first composer of international standing produced by Britain for nearly two

centuries, but since his day a steady stream of British composers has poured forth a variety of music sophisticatedly European in its provenance, popular in performance and wholly British in its melodic freshness, harmonic lucidity and ironic wit. And while British composers have been forging their new reputation, British performers have made even more dramatic strides. In the 1920s, there were four permanent professional symphony orchestras in Britain; in the 1980s, there were 17. At least as many smaller groups of comparably high standard, mostly private in origin and often specializing in certain kinds of music, have sprung up since World War II. The adaptability and artistic independence of these groups are the envy of the more traditionally organized music professions of other European countries: their repertoire is more adventurous and their members less tied to established symphony orchestras, opera houses and teaching institutions.

In the musical sphere, the British insistence on choice has become danger-

Confidently decked in an eclectic variety of garments, a leader of the avant-garde fashion world of the 1980s (below) makes her contribution to the onward march of style. Other adherents of various trends, from punk to neo-romantic, sport outré hairstyles as the badge of their allegiance.

ously luxurious. Everyone agrees that London's four full-sized symphony orchestras are at least one too many to extract the best from the money, audience and talent available. With the resources spread so widely, London has failed to produce any single orchestra on the level of those of, for example, Chicago, Vienna or Berlin. None of the four, however, will put its head on the block, and each weakening candidate recovers miraculously in time before its audiences and sponsors vanish and its grant is cut off.

Alone among the theatrical and musical capitals of the world, London never closes. Theatres play 12 months of the year; first nights continue through August—unheard of in Paris or New York. July sees a music festival in the City of London, August another on the South Bank. Outside London there is a steady calendar of local and international concert and opera seasons from April to October, from Bath and Brighton in the south to the Orkney Isles, north of Scotland, where the composer Peter Maxwell Davies

directs the St. Magnus Festival, which mixes local performers with international stars. Edinburgh, first in the field after the Second World War, remains simply the largest and the most comprehensive festival of music and drama throughout the world. Alongside the official festival, which receives funds from the city, the Arts Council and private sponsors, an unsubsidized "fringe" of more experimental productions flourishes, threatening to surpass some of the main festival in quality as well as variety.

The Edinburgh Festival attracts close to one million and the London theatre around two million foreign visitors each year. For people who never leave home, however, Britain's cultural presence is felt in the work of its distinguished writers and, more pervasively, through the international success of British broadcasting and pop music, in which fields the nation retains a world influence. They have nothing else in common: British broadcasting stands for probity and imagination; British

6

pop flirts with decadence and taboo.

British popular music has sustained its international pre-eminence for more than two decades since the arrival of the Beatles and the Rolling Stones. The world buys it not merely for the words and music it wants to hear, but for the implied cultural attitudes behind them. Singers like Mick Jagger, Rod Stewart, David Bowie, Elton John, Sting and Boy George articulate individual aggressiveness and eccentricity, sexual ambivalence, bad taste and fun.

The British Broadcasting Company, later Corporation, was founded in 1922. From the start, it was financed by a licence fee levied on households that received its broadcasts. It has thus been independent of direct government control, though subject to ceaseless pressures both subtle and coarse from politicians, trade unionists and the public, who express their opinions through the rating figures. The BBC is bound by charter to remain entirely impartial in its presentation of news and current affairs. How far it succeeds in this may be seen from the fact that left-wing socialists consider that the BBC is run by members of the Tory establishment, and some Conservatives that it is clearly the Trotskyite vanguard of revolution to come.

In its early days, the BBC quickly mastered the art of sound broadcasting, and its authoritative programmes quickly established a loyal audience that still exists today. Its classical music broadcasts have been particularly influential—indeed, the BBC has been the greatest single force behind the remarkable renaissance of music in 20th-century Britain. BBC's Radio 3, the classical music programme, has an eclectic and ever-expanding repertory; six of the nation's large-scale

Exhausted visitors take a rest from the mêlée at the opening of the Royal Academy's Summer Exhibition. From thousands of works submitted by professional and amateur artists, the Academy's committee selects some 1,500 for the three-month show.

orchestras are managed by the BBC.

The most famous contribution to the nation's musical life by the BBC is the series of Promenade Concerts which run at London's Royal Albert Hall for eight weeks every summer. Broadcast complete on Radio 3, the "Proms" add up to the longest and greatest music festival in the world. The range of music is extraordinary; listeners may be presented with anything from an Indonesian gamelan band to a complete rendering of Berlioz's mammoth opera *The Trojans*. For the concerts, the seats are removed from the stalls of the Albert Hall, and the arena is filled with a young, standing audience paying very low prices. The most austere of soloists accept hearty youthful irreverence and ironic cheers before the music starts; once it does, they hold the audience spellbound. The feast of the Proms is made possible by state funding of the BBC: no private body could possibly afford it.

The BBC began transmitting the world's first high-definition television

service as early as 1936. It was shut down during the Second World War, but restarted in 1946. At first it was not a resounding success: its diet of jolly quiz shows and its educational tone lacked the superb confidence of the radio service. But already by the 1950s it was showing glimpses of the brilliance it would reveal later.

Since 1955, independent television—independent, that is, of both the government and the BBC—has provided an alternative service, run by commercial interests and supported by advertising on the screen. Franchises for 15 areas of Britain are allotted every 10 years by an overall authority that answers neither to the government nor to the commercial interests. The franchise companies produce and feed their own programmes into the ITV network. Since 1982, they have in addition contributed according to their wealth to a second ITV programme, Channel 4, which is designed also as a forum for independent producers.

Although BBC television had a head start, ITV has, since the early 1960s, consistently attracted more viewers than the BBC, chiefly with soap operas that follow the American pattern but draw on the timeless fabric of British life. Its greatest popular success has been *Coronation Street*, set in a district of Victorian "back-to-back" houses (with only a narrow passage between two terraces) somewhere in Manchester. It is a secular world of gossip, generosity, convention and adaptability; pub and corner shop have replaced the church and chapel of an earlier generation as social foci. The observation is acute, the detail accurate, offering the closeness of a traditional community but moving cannily and responsively with the times. The mixture of the nostalgic

Under the baton of the conductor on his streamer-festooned podium, the audience filling London's Albert Hall sings Elgar's patriotic ode "Land of Hope and Glory"—the climactic ritual that invariably closes the last night of the BBC's Promenade Concert season.

and the actual strikes at the heart of the British subconscious. First broadcast in 1963, *Coronation Street* still attracts between 12 and 16 million viewers twice weekly.

In the mid-1960s, television began to reach the heights earlier attained by radio, and since then the British have enjoyed a television service that many rate the best in any country. The BBC is a master of scholarly popularization and champion of contemporary drama. Both the BBC and ITV produce memorable historical and classic drama series that sell all round the world. The quality stems from the BBC's tradition of public service. Freed from the need to make a profit, it has had time to grow and explore. Its ethos of excellence has been so strong that ITV was forced to emulate and then surpass it in order to make an impact.

To generate their superb output, the BBC and ITV draw upon all that is most positive in the nation's artistic life. Much of the best British acting, writing, directing and producing talent has worked in television. Taking their sustenance out of the British talent pool, the BBC and ITV put at least as much back in: the work they provide makes them immensely important patrons of the arts.

With so much creativity channelled into television, and with Hollywood long established as the aggressive world centre of the film industry, British cinema has sometimes seemed a fragile plant. Yet it has enjoyed two boom periods in the past three decades. The first came in the late 1950s and early 1960s, when films like *Room at the Top* and *Saturday Night and Sunday Morning* offered unfamiliar glimpses of life in industrial northern England and attracted the big American market. After these successes, new writers, actors and directors emerged in droves.

American distributors fastened on to the apparently inexhaustible source of talent and ideas, and for a few years money flowed from the United States into the laps of British directors. But the distributors' enthusiasm eventually

Britain's record of achievement in literature is unparalleled. Besides William Shakespeare, whose plays could, by themselves, stand for Britain's cultural heritage until the end of time, the nation has produced scores of poets, novelists, essayists and dramatists of genius. Britain has never been a world leader in music or the visual arts, but has still produced many notable exponents in these fields. On these two pages, some of the most outstanding creators and thinkers the nation has produced are listed in chronological order.

ARCHITECTURE AND DESIGN

Inigo Jones	1573–1652
Christopher Wren	1632–1723
Nicholas Hawksmoor	1661–1736
John Vanbrugh	1664–1726
James Gibbs	1682–1754
William Kent	1684–1748
William Caslon	1692–1766
Lord Burlington	1694–1753
John Baskerville	1706–1775
Lancelot "Capability" Brown	1716–1783
Thomas Chippendale	1718–1779
George Hepplewhite	died 1786
Robert Adam	1728–1792
James Adam	1730–1794
Josiah Wedgwood	1730–1795
James Wyatt	1746–1813
Thomas Sheraton	1751–1806
Humphrey Repton	1752–1818
John Nash	1752–1835
John Soane	1753–1837
Josiah Spode	1754–1827
Charles Barry	1795–1860
Joseph Paxton	1803–1865
Isambard Kingdom Brunel	1806–1859
George Gilbert Scott	1811–1878
Augustus Pugin	1812–1852
William Butterfield	1814–1900
Richard Norman Shaw	1831–1912
William Morris	1834–1896
Charles Annesley Voysey	1857–1941
Charles Rennie Mackintosh	1868–1928
Edwin Lutyens	1869–1944

PAINTING AND SCULPTURE

Nicholas Hilliard	1547–1619
Isaac Oliver	c. 1550–1617
Grinling Gibbons	1648–1721
William Hogarth	1697–1764
Richard Wilson	1714–1782
Sir Joshua Reynolds	1723–1792
George Stubbs	1724–1806
Thomas Gainsborough	1727–1788
Joseph Wright	1734–1797
J. R. Cozens	1752–1797
John Flaxman	1755–1826
Sir Henry Raeburn	1756–1823
Thomas Rowlandson	1756–1827
Thomas Lawrence	1769–1830
William Turner	1775–1851
John Constable	1776–1837
John Sell Cotman	1782–1842
Richard Bonington	1802–1828
Edwin Landseer	1802–1873
Samuel Palmer	1805–1881
Ford Madox Brown	1821–1893
William Holman Hunt	1827–1910
Dante Gabriel Rossetti	1828–1882
John Everett Millais	1829–1896
Edward Burne-Jones	1833–1898
Walter Sickert	1860–1942
Arthur Rackham	1867–1939
Aubrey Beardsley	1872–1898
Augustus John	1878–1961
Jacob Epstein	1880–1959
Paul Nash	1889–1946
Stanley Spencer	1891–1959
Ben Nicholson	1894–1982
Barbara Hepworth	1903–1975
Graham Sutherland	1903–1980

The critic John Ruskin, painted by Millais.

PHILOSOPHY AND RELIGION

Thomas More	1478–1535
Francis Bacon	1561–1626
Thomas Hobbes	1588–1679
John Locke	1632–1704
George Berkeley	1685–1753
David Hume	1711–1776
Adam Smith	1723–1790
Edmund Burke	1729–1797
Jeremy Bentham	1748–1832
William Godwin	1757–1836
John Henry Newman	1801–1890
John Stuart Mill	1806–1873
Herbert Spencer	1820–1903
Alfred North Whitehead	1861–1947
Bertrand Russell	1872–1970
George Edward Moore	1873–1958

MUSIC

Thomas Tallis	c. 1505–1585
William Byrd	c. 1543–1623
Giles Farnaby	c. 1560–1640
John Bull	c. 1562–1628
John Dowland	c. 1563–1626
Orlando Gibbons	1583–1625
Henry Purcell	c. 1659–1695
Thomas Arne	1710–1778
Arthur Sullivan	1842–1900
Edward Elgar	1857–1934
Frederick Delius	1862–1934
Ralph Vaughan Williams	1872–1958
Gustav Holst	1874–1934
Ivor Novello	1893–1951
Gerald Finzi	1901–1956
William Walton	1902–1983
Benjamin Britten	1913–1976

LITERATURE AND DRAMA

William Langland	c. 1330–1400
Geoffrey Chaucer	c. 1345–1400
Thomas Malory	c. 1400–1471
Edmund Spenser	c. 1552–1599
Philip Sidney	1554–1586
Thomas Kyd	c. 1558–1594
Christopher Marlowe	1564–1593
William Shakespeare	1564–1616
Thomas Middleton	c. 1570–1627
John Donne	c. 1571–1631
Ben Jonson	1572–1637
John Fletcher	1579–1625
John Webster	c. 1580–1625
Francis Beaumont	1584–1616
Robert Herrick	1591–1674
George Herbert	1593–1633
Izaak Walton	1593–1683
Thomas Browne	1605–1682
John Milton	1608–1674
John Evelyn	1620–1706
Andrew Marvell	1621–1678
John Bunyan	1628–1688
John Dryden	1631–1700
Samuel Pepys	1633–1703
Daniel Defoe	c. 1660–1731

The novelist Charlotte Brontë.

Jonathan Swift	1667–1745
William Congreve	1670–1729
Joseph Addison	1672–1719
John Gay	1685–1732
Alexander Pope	1688–1744
Samuel Richardson	1689–1761
Henry Fielding	1707–1754
Samuel Johnson	1709–1784
Laurence Sterne	1713–1768
Horace Walpole	1717–1794
Tobias Smollett	1721–1771
Oliver Goldsmith	c. 1730–1774
William Cowper	1731–1800
Edward Gibbon	1737–1794
James Boswell	1740–1795
Richard Brinsley Sheridan	1751–1816
William Blake	1757–1827
Robert Burns	1759–1796
William Wordsworth	1770–1850
Walter Scott	1771–1832
Samuel Taylor Coleridge	1772–1834
Jane Austen	1775–1817
Charles Lamb	1775–1834
Thomas de Quincey	1785–1859
Lord Byron	1788–1824
Percy Bysshe Shelley	1792–1822
Thomas Carlyle	1795–1881
John Keats	1795–1821
Thomas Babington Macaulay	1800–1859
Elizabeth Barrett Browning	1806–1861
Alfred Lord Tennyson	1809–1892
Elizabeth Gaskell	1810–1865
William Makepeace Thackeray	1811–1863
Charles Dickens	1812–1870
Edward Lear	1812–1888
Robert Browning	1812–1889
Anthony Trollope	1815–1882
Charlotte Brontë	1816–1855
Emily Brontë	1818–1848
George Eliot	1819–1880
John Ruskin	1819–1900
Anne Brontë	1820–1849
Richard Burton	1821–1890
Matthew Arnold	1822–1888
Lewis Carroll	1832–1898
Samuel Butler	1835–1902
Algernon Charles Swinburne	1837–1909
Thomas Hardy	1840–1928
Gerard Manley Hopkins	1844–1889
Robert Louis Stevenson	1850–1894
Oscar Wilde	1854–1900
George Bernard Shaw	1856–1950
Joseph Conrad	1857–1924
Arthur Conan Doyle	1859–1930
A. E. Housman	1859–1936
Rudyard Kipling	1865–1936
W. B. Yeats	1865–1939
H. G. Wells	1866–1946
Arnold Bennett	1867–1931
John Galsworthy	1867–1933
Ford Madox Ford	1873–1939
G. K. Chesterton	1874–1936
Somerset Maugham	1874–1965

John Masefield	1878–1967
E. M. Forster	1879–1970
Lytton Strachey	1880–1932
P. G. Wodehouse	1881–1975
Virginia Woolf	1882–1941
D. H. Lawrence	1885–1930
Rupert Brooke	1887–1915
T. S. Eliot	1888–1965
Hugh McDiarmid	1892–1978
Wilfred Owen	1893–1918
Aldous Huxley	1894–1963
Noël Coward	1899–1973
George Orwell	1903–1950
Evelyn Waugh	1903–1966
John Betjeman	1906–1984
W. H. Auden	1907–1973
Dylan Thomas	1914–1953
Paul Scott	1920–1978

Oscar Wilde, the dramatist, essayist and wit.

The gift of God is eternal life

outran their judgement, and they found themselves with some expensive failures on their hands. By the early 1970s, a reaction had set in and American funds were drying up. Meanwhile the indigenous cinema was becoming less and less capable of surviving without outside markets: with the growth of television, cinemas were closing daily, and at the start of the 1970s the number of cinemas open in the whole of Britain equalled those open in the London area alone a quarter of a century earlier.

When the 1960s boom faded, British studios and technicians—among the best-equipped and most talented in the world—were hired out to American and multinational production companies, and many of the greatest box-office successes of the 1970s and early 1980s,

including the James Bond, Superman and Star Wars series, were British.

By the early 1980s, although cinema audience figures in Britain were still plummeting, videos were selling in enormous numbers to British households, creating a new audience for films. That factor, together with the arrival of the fourth television channel and rise of the independent producer, brought a spark of life back to the domestic British film industry. Between 1979 and 1984, generous tax allowances removed some of the risk from film-making and encouraged British investors to put money into films. Their first big reward came in 1982 when *Chariots of Fire*—the story of two gold medallists at the 1924 Olympic Games—won the Oscar for Best Pic-

ture at America's annual Academy Award presentations for cinematic excellence. A year later, another British film—*Gandhi*—repeated that success. At last there were good prospects for a thriving domestic film industry, which was to some extent dependent on the American market, but not its slave either artistically or financially.

The British press has seen as many vicissitudes as the film industry and has been pronounced terminally sick on countless occasions. However, the British still buy and read more newspapers per capita of the population than most other nations. They are much more likely to buy a national than a local newspaper: unlike most developed nations, Britain has its press centred in the capital. Indeed, most of the 10

152

In an indoor market in the West Country city of Bath, a stallholder dozes among his accumulation of relics. Valuable or not, most objects from bygone eras will sooner or later find a buyer in one of the junk shops that abound throughout the country.

A bookseller who works from an open-air stall takes advantage of a slack moment to assess some recent acquisitions. The trade in secondhand books is brisk at all levels, from ordinary titles for the general reader to rare antiquarian volumes that change hands through specialist dealers.

national dailies and eight national Sunday newspapers are produced in or close to a single thoroughfare, Fleet Street, just west of the City of London.

Fleet Street's besetting problem is its industrial relations. Over the years, weak managements have effectively ceded power over their print rooms to the unions. As a result, restrictive practices and overmanning are rife, and labour-saving technology is resisted. Few newspapers are in the pink of health: most are owned by large industrial groups and subsidized by the more efficient sides of the business.

In a scramble for profits, the newspapers are engaged in intense competition for circulation and advertising revenue—competition that lowers standards rather than raising them. The tabloid newspapers that cater for a mass readership aim for large sales by entertaining with sport, sex, royalty and television chat. Guidance on serious issues is minimal. An independent Royal Commission on the press, which published its findings in 1977, revealed that in the mass daily newspapers sport occupied between one third and one half of the news space, while foreign affairs were squeezed into less than 20 per cent—sometimes much less—and the space allocated to "parliamentary debate reports" was nil.

The serious newspapers, by comparison, are very good indeed. They provide more thorough news cover and analysis than radio and television, and a number, including *The Times*, the *Guardian* and the *Financial Times*, have an international standing. News magazines of the type of *Time*, *Der Spiegel* and *L'Express* do not exist in Britain, but *The Economist*—which ranges far more widely over current affairs than its title implies—enjoys a high repu-

tation as a journal of opinion both in Britain and abroad.

Book publishing, likewise and thanks partly to the commercial success of television-orientated titles, is resourceful and resilient. The American market is essential for most British book publishers, but the British are enthusiastic readers too: surveys over the last few years have regularly found 45 per cent of those questioned to be currently reading a book.

In the 1960s, the novel seemed to be in decline in Britain: the temptations of other media, especially theatre and television, proved too seductive to enterprising writers. But in the 1970s and 1980s, although the other media continued to exert their lure, more and more British writers returned to prose fiction. Only a few well-reviewed titles sell more than 10,000 copies, and the majority far fewer—between 2,000 and 5,000. Yet poor financial rewards seem no deterrent, and gifted novelists continue to spring up. Their talent is supported by a handful of editors and agents committed to fiction, by promotional campaigns in the trade and by a large annual cash prize given by the Booker McConnell company that, with the help of newspapers and TV, generates publicity not only for the prize-winner but for new novels in general.

Rather than buy a book, however, the British prefer to borrow through the extensive public library system. In the early 1980s, total borrowing amounted to more than 10 books annually per capita of population. While in the United States one book was borrowed for every one purchased, in Britain the ratio was 15 to one. The library system stretches from the big cities and suburbs to vans, operated by the local authorities, that travel the highlands

and islands and moors at Britain's edge: it suffered from inflation in the 1970s and from cuts in the 1980s, but it remains one of the best, and best-used, in the world.

Authors have naturally resented the loss in sales that results from library loans and they have campaigned vigorously for just recompense. For years they made little progress, but in 1979 the Public Lending Right Bill became law. Under its provisions, government funds are distributed to authors in proportion to the number of times their books have been borrowed from a representative sample of public libraries. The first payments, made in 1984, would not have revolutionized the authors' lifestyles. Of the £2 million set aside for the scheme, more than

In a field in Buckinghamshire, a white-clad troupe threads the intricate maze of a Morris dance—a folk dance of ancient origin once connected with magical fertility rites. Enthusiastic teams of Morris men keep the tradition alive in most English counties.

£400,000 went on operating costs; the rest was distributed between more than 6,000 authors, the majority of whom received less than £100; 46 authors received the top payment of £5,000.

Whether borrowed or bought, the books most commonly read in Britain reflect the nation's broad cultural preoccupations: sport, cookery, gardening, antique collecting, the Royal Family, dieting and health; most strikingly, the countryside and everyday life in the past. Few books of the post-war period have enjoyed such popularity as Laurie Lee's *Cider with Rosie* (1959), the autobiography of a Cotswold country childhood. And in the late 1970s, *The Country Diary of an Edwardian Lady*—a charmingly illustrated, handwritten anthology of seasonal sayings and verse—became a publishing and merchandising phenomenon which far outstripped the modest if pleasing talents of the lady who had left it behind.

The British are in thrall to the past and to enduring traditions (like royalty) in ways both profound and trivial. The obsession cuts across all levels of income and taste. Revealed clearly in the public's choice of reading matter, it is manifest too in the work of playwrights such as Osborne and in the viewing public's addiction to the timeless, close-knit community of *Coronation Street*. Disorientated by their nation's changing place in the world and by the blurring of hierarchies within their society, the British look back in search of certainties, comfort and reassurance.

The British landscape, so full of history, is treasured as a link with the past. A vocal lobby campaigns against almost any change wrought by farmers in search of higher profits. Stretches of countryside totalling 9 per cent of England and Wales have been designated National Parks; the land remains in private hands, but stringent controls on development prevent the destruction of the areas' beauty. Thirteen per cent of Scotland's total land area is similarly protected.

Equally, the British cherish their architecture of the past. The government's list of buildings of special architectural or historical interest has more than 300,000 entries and it is still growing. It is against the law to demolish or alter the character of any listed build-

ing without special permission, which is not often forthcoming.

Individuals can show their concern for the nation's heritage by joining the National Trust, a private environmental body set up at the turn of the century to buy and conserve buildings and land otherwise threatened by demolition or development. The National Trust now has well over a million members and is the third largest landowner in Britain after the Church and the Crown.

The British tradition of caring for the objects of the past is a long one, and it is not parochial. In the 18th and 19th centuries, British archaeologists and antiquaries dug up and recorded much of ancient Italy, Greece and the Near East, bringing many of their finds back with them to London. The museums which house these and other treasures were funded by the state long before the Arts Council was set up to subsidize the performing arts. Today they remain among the finest in the world, and they are well attended; special exhibitions draw immense crowds.

Recently the British have even come to embrace their industrial past. Ever since Arnold deplored the philistinism of the profiteers, many in Britain have felt a moral distaste for the dirty hands of trade. But once machinery becomes old and no longer makes money, it is received with something near love. The National Trust has begun to concern itself with industrial buildings. Railway museums have sprung up—the British, having developed the world's first rail network, virtually invented railway mania when it began to run down.

The most influential museum to be opened in Britain in the 1970s, inspiring a revival of interest in local history throughout the country, was the Ironbridge Gorge Museum in Shropshire.

In a 5-square-kilometre area in the comparatively rustic valley of the Severn River, the museum encompasses six early industrial sites, including Coalbrookdale, the cradle of the Industrial Revolution, where iron ore was first smelted with coke in 1709. The original furnace is on view today; nearby are the world's first cast-iron bridge, dating from 1779, 19th-century tile and china works, and a whole early industrial community—the houses of iron-masters and men, together with their chapels, schools, shops and pubs. Hundreds of thousands of visitors each year are overcome with nostalgia for this re-created world.

Nostalgia was a new word coined in the 18th century—when it meant simply home-sickness, usually suffered for Britain in the American colonies or the Far East. After the Second World War, the word was enfeebled to convey merely the trivial escape from a present in which Britain no longer enjoyed a leading political and economic role. Now, however, nostalgia is being re-defined again so that it can accommodate the honouring of ancestors and the awareness of positive qualities in the British temperament and past achievements—a metaphorical homesickness. Ironbridge Gorge Museum is a home-coming, and in an increasing number of similar explorations all over the land, the British are starting to return to their roots. If their quest is not always for "the best that has been known and said in the world", as Matthew Arnold intended, it still amounts to a painstaking redefinition of culture itself. Broadened to include nostalgia in its noblest sense, culture has at last acquired the power to fill the whole nation, including the philistines, with the passion for sweetness and light.

A gardener in a Cambridge college shaves the turf to a velvet nap. In Britain's cool, moist climate, where grass grows reliably, lawns can be brought to a pitch of perfection in public parks and the grounds of stately homes—and in a million suburban front gardens.

ACKNOWLEDGEMENTS

The index for this book was prepared by Vicki Robinson. For their help in the preparation of this volume, the editors wish to thank: Richard Addis, London; Arts Council of Great Britain, London; Earl of Bradford, Shropshire; British Broadcasting Company, London; British Library, London; British Phonographic Industry, London; Mike Brown, London; Mick Brunton, London; Department of Trade and Industry, London; Louise Earwaker, London; Gordon Heald, Gallup Polls, London; Elizabeth Hodgson, North Yorkshire; Peter and Brenda Hopkins, Chester; Jay Hornsby, London; Independent Schools Information Service, London; Elizabeth Jones, Ferranti, Manchester; Christopher Ledger, Shell U.K. Exploration and Production, London; Philip Mason, Hampshire; Thomas Milan, London; Russell Miller, Buckinghamshire; National Trust, London; Office of Population Censuses and Surveys, London; Royal Horticultural Society, London; Royal Library, Windsor; Science Museum Library, London.

PICTURE CREDITS

Credits from left to right are separated by semicolons, from top to bottom by dashes.

Cover: Denis Waugh, London. Front endpaper: Map by Roger Stewart, London. Back endpaper: Digitized image by Creative Data, London.

1, 2: © Flag Research Center, Winchester, Massachusetts. 6, 7: Patrick Thurston, London, digitized chart by Creative Data. 8, 9: M. A. Bennett from Colorific!, London. Digitized image by Creative Data, London. 10, 11: Patrick Ward, London, Digitized image by Creative Data, London, 12, 13: Julian Calder, London, 14, 15: National Coal Board, London, digitized chart by Creative Data. 16, 17: Derry Brabbs from Images Colour Library Ltd., Leeds, England. 18, 19: Michael Freeman, London. 20: Homer Sykes, London; Camerapix Hutchison Library, London; Patrick Ward, London. 21: David Simson, Bisley, England. 22: Ray Duffurn from Fotobank International Colour Library, London. 23: Rob Cousins from Susan Griggs Agency, London. 24: Patrick Thurston, London. 27: David Beatty, Bath, England. 29: Adam Woolfitt from Susan Griggs Agency, London. 30, 31: Homer Sykes, London. 32: Cary Wolinsky from Stock, Boston, U.S.A. 33: Homer Sykes, London; Liam White, London—Homer Sykes, London. 34–37: Derry Brabbs from Images Colour Library, Ltd., Leeds, England. 38: Colin Molyneux, Caerphilly, Wales. 39: Derek Widdicombe, Huddersfield, England—Adam Woolfitt from Susan Griggs Agency, London. 40, 41: Patrick Ward, London. 42: Anthony Howarth from Susan Griggs

Agency, London. 43: David Simson, Bisley, England. 44: Illustration from the Wriothesley Manuscript. Copyright reserved. Reproduced by Gracious Permission of Her Majesty The Queen. 46: Detail from Ms. Cotton Claudius B4, f 59, The British Library, London. 47: By courtesy of Hungerford Church, photo Julian Calder, London. 48: Peter Jackson Collection, London. 49: Reproduced by courtesy of the trustees of the British Museum, London, photo Ray Gardener, London. 50: Liam White, London. 51: The British Museum Collection of Personal and Political Satires, engraving no. 858. 52: Sutton Hoo Helmet, reproduced by courtesy of the trustees of the British Museum, London, photo E.T. Archive, London; collotype courtesy of the Guildhall Library, London. 53: Miniature by Nicholas Hilliard, 1581, courtesy of the National Portrait Gallery, London; courtesy of the Royal Society, London, photo E.T. Archive, London— Liverpool and Manchester Railway from Mary Evans Picture Library, London. 54: E.T. Archive, London; Imperial War Museum, London. 55: Watercolour by Robert Dighton courtesy of the Museum of London. 56: Digitized image by Creative Data, London—engraving from Cassell's *Old and New London* c. 1876 from the Peter Jackson Collection, London. 58: Adam Woolfitt from the Daily Telegraph Colour Library, London. 60: Adam Woolfitt from Susan Griggs Agency, London. 61: Mauro Carraro from Rex Features, London. 62, 63: Laurie Lewis, London. 64: Jubilee commemorative portrait 1897, E.T. Archive, London—BBC Hulton Picture Library, London; Mansell Collection, London—portrait by Bryan Organ, 1981, courtesy of National Portrait Gallery, London; portrait by Annigoni by kind permission of the Fishmongers' Company, London. 65: Mansell Collection, London. 66, 67: The Photo Source, London. 68, 69: Mark Cator, London. 70–72: Patrick Ward, London. 74: Julian Calder, London. 76: Patrick Ward, London. 77: Julian Calder, London. 78: Romano Cagnoni, London. 79: Homer Sykes, London. 81: Ray Green, Cheadle, Cheshire, England. 83: Romano Cagnoni, London. 84: Patrick Ward from Susan Griggs Agency, London. 85: Patrick Ward, London. 87: Cary Wolinsky from Stock, Boston, U.S.A. 88, 89: Patrick Thurston, London. 90, 91: Mark Cator, London. 92: Patrick Ward, London (2). 93: Patrick Ward from Susan Griggs Agency, London (2). 94, 95: Patrick Ward, London. 96, 97: Julian Calder, London. 98, 99: The Photo Source, London. 101: Illustrated London News photo, Mary Evans Picture Library, London. 103: Sport and General Press Agency Ltd., London. 104: Patrick Eagar, Kew, England. 106: Laurie Lewis, London; Patrick Ward, London (2). 108, 109: Popperfoto, London. 110: Digitized image by Creative Data, London. 112: Julian Calder, London. 114: Digitized image by

Creative Data, London. 115: Richard Robinson from Images Colour Library Ltd., Leeds, England. 116: David Beatty from Susan Griggs Agency, London. 117: Derry Brabbs from Images Colour Library Ltd., Leeds, England. 118: Patrick Thurston, London; Adam Woolfitt from Susan Griggs Agency, London—Patrick Ward, London. 119: Derek Widdicombe, Huddersfield, England (3). 121: Julian Calder, London, courtesy of Oxford Instruments Group plc. 123: Homer Sykes, London. 124: Michael Freeman, London. 125: Adam Woolfitt from Susan Griggs Agency, London. 126: Illustrations from *The History of the Twelve Great Livery Companies of London*, 1836. 127, 128: Michael Freeman, London. 130–137: Michael St. Maur Sheil from Susan Griggs Agency, London, except illustration 132, Oxford Illustrators Ltd. 138–141: Patrick Ward, London. 142: Homer Sykes, London. 143: Julian Calder, London. 144, 145: Patrick Ward, London. 146: Ben Gibson, Bristol, England; Pete Wilkie, London; Terence Spencer, London. 147: David Simson, Bisley, England; Pete Wilkie, London; Terence Spencer, London. 148: Patrick Ward, London. 149: Frank Herrmann from Colorific!, London. 150: Portrait by Millais from a private collection. 151: Portrait by G. Richmond, 1850, courtesy of the National Portrait Gallery, London; portrait by Carlo Pellegrini, 1884, courtesy of the National Portrait Gallery, London. 152, 153: David Beatty, Bath, England. 154: Homer Sykes, London. 155: Alva Bernadine, London.

BIBLIOGRAPHY

BOOKS
Ardagh, John, *A Tale of Five Cities*. Secker and Warburg, London, 1979.
Arnold, Matthew, *Culture and Anarchy*. Cambridge University Press, Cambridge, 1932.
Bagehot, Walter, *The English Constitution*. Fontana, London, 1963.
Barnett, Correlli, *The Collapse of British Power*. Eyre Methuen, London, 1972.
Barr, Ann, and York, Peter, *The Official Sloane Ranger Handbook*. Ebury Press, London, 1982. *The Official Sloane Ranger Diary*. Ebury Press, London, 1983.
Beer, Samuel H., *Britain Against Itself*. Faber and Faber, London, 1982.
Beloff, Max, *Imperial Sunset: Britain's Liberal Empire 1897–1921*. Methuen, London, 1969.
Beloff, Max, and Peele, Gillian, *The Government of the United Kingdom*. Weidenfeld and Nicolson, London, 1980.
Bradley, Ian, *The English Middle Classes are Alive*

and Kicking. Collins, London, 1982.
Briggs, Asa: *A Social History of England*.
Weidenfeld and Nicolson, London, 1983.
The Age of Improvement. Longman, London,
1959.
*The History of Broadcasting in the United Kingdom.
Vols. 1–4*. Oxford University Press, Oxford,
1961–1979.
Bromley, John F., *The Armorial Bearings of the
Guilds of London*. Frederick Warne, London,
1960.
Burt, Alfred Leroy, *The Evolution of the British
Empire and Commonwealth from the American
Revolution*. D. C. Heath, 1956.
Butt, John, and Donnachie, Ian, *Industrial
Archaeology in the British Isles*. Paul Elek,
London, 1979.
Butt, Philip Alan, *The Welsh Question*. University
of Wales Press, Cardiff, 1975.
Churchill, Winston S., *The Island Race*. Cassell,
London, 1964.
Coates, B. E., and Rawstron, E. M., *Regional
Variations in Britain*. Batsford, London, 1971.
Cross, Colin, *The Fall of the British Empire*. Hodder
and Stoughton, Sevenoaks, Kent, 1968.
Cuddon, J. A., *The Macmillan Dictionary of Sport
and Games*. Macmillan Press, Basingstoke,
Hants, 1980.
Dahrendorf, Ralph, *On Britain*. British
Broadcasting Corporation, London, 1980.
Dalyell, Ram, *Devolution: The End of Britain*.
Jonathan Cape, London, 1977.
Downing, Taylor, ed., *The Troubles*. Thames
Macdonald Futura, 1980.
Drabble, Margaret, *A Writer's Britain*. Thames
and Hudson, London, 1979.
Eaton, J., and Gill, C., *Trade Union Directory*.
Pluto Press, London, 1981.
Elliston Allen D., *British Tastes*. Penguin Books,
London, 1968.
Engels, Frederick, *The Condition of the Working
Class in England in 1844*. Blackwell, Oxford,
1971.
Falconer, Keith: *Guide to England's Industrial
Heritage*. Batsford, London, 1980.
A History of England. Macmillan, London, 1950.
Findlater, Richard, *Lilian Baylis*. Allen Lane,
London, 1975.
Goldthorpe, John H., *Social Mobility and Class
Structure in Modern Britain*. Clarendon Press,
Oxford, 1980.
Goldthorpe, John H., et al: *The Affluent Worker.
The Affluent Worker in the Class Structure.
Industrial Attitudes and Behaviour*. Cambridge
University Press, Cambridge, 1968.
Gordon, D. C., *The Moment of Power. Britain's
Imperial Epoch*. Prentice-Hall, New Jersey,
1970.
Graham, Gerald S., *A Concise History of the British
Empire*. Thames and Hudson, London, 1970.
Greene, Graham, ed., *The Old School Tie*.
Jonathan Cape, London, 1934.

Grierson, Edward, *The Imperial Dream*. Collins,
London, 1972.
Halsey, A. H., *Change in British Society*. Oxford
University Press, Oxford, 1978.
Halsey, A. H., ed., *Trends in British Society since
1900*. Macmillan, Basingstoke, Hants, 1972.
Halsey, A. H., Heath, A. F., and Ridge, J. M.,
Origins and Destinations. Clarendon Press,
Oxford, 1980.
Hanson, A. H., and Walles, M., *Governing Britain*.
Fontana, London, 1970.
Harrison, Paul, *Inside the Inner City*. Penguin
Books, London, 1983.
Hartnoll, Phyllis, ed., *The Concise Oxford
Companion to the Theatre*. Oxford University
Press, Oxford, 1978.
Harvey, Sir Paul, *The Oxford Companion to English
Literature*. Oxford University Press, Oxford,
1975.
Heath, Anthony, *Social Mobility*. Fontana,
London, 1981.
Herbert, William, *History of the Twelve Great Livery
Companies of London. Vols. 1 & 2*. Published by
the author, c. 1836.
Hill, Christopher, *The Century of Revolution 1603–
1714*. Nelson, Walton-on-Thames, Surrey,
1961.
Hobsbawm, E. J., *Industry and Empire*. Weidenfeld
and Nicolson, London, 1969.
Hoggart, Richard: *The Uses of Literacy*. Chatto &
Windus, London, 1957.
An English Temper. Chatto & Windus, London,
1982.
Hooberman, Ben, *An Introduction to British Trade
Unions*. Penguin Books, London, 1974.
Horne, Donald, *God is an Englishman*, Angus &
Robertson, London, 1970.
Hoskins, W. G., *The Making of the English
Landscape*. Penguin Books, London, 1970.
Kellas, James G., *The Scottish Political System*.
Cambridge University Press, Cambridge, 1975.
Lacey, Robert, *Majesty*. Hutchinson, London,
1977.
Lane, Peter, *The Upper Class*. Batsford, London,
1972.
Levin, Bernard, *The Pendulum Years: Britain and the
Sixties*. Jonathan Cape, London, 1970.
Macaulay, Thomas Babington, *The History of
England*. J. M. Dent, London, 1906.
Macinnes, Colin, *Sweet Saturday Night*.
MacGibbon and Kee, London, 1967.
Marwick, Arthur: *British Society since 1945*.
Pelican, London, 1982.
*Class: Image and Reality in Britain, France and the
U.S.A. since 1930*. Collins, London, 1980.
Melly, George, *Revolt into Style: The Pop Arts in
Britain*. Allen Lane, London, 1970.
Middlemass, Keith, *Politics in Industrial Society*.
André Deutsch, London, 1979.
Morris, James, *Farewell the Trumpets. Heaven's
Command. Pax Britannica*. Penguin Books,
London, 1982.

Nairn, Tom C., *The Break-Up of Britain*. New Left
Books, London, 1977.
Nicolson, James R., *Shetland*. David and Charles,
Newton Abbot, Devon, 1972.
Nossiter, Bernard, *Britain—A Future that Works*.
André Deutsch, London, 1978.
Nutting, Anthony, *No End of a Lesson: The Story of
Suez*. Constable, London, 1967.
Orwell, George, *Homage to Catalonia*. Penguin
Books, London, 1969.
*The English People from The Collected Essays,
Journals and Letters of George Orwell. Vol. 3*.
Penguin Books, London, 1970.
Osborne, Harold, *The Oxford Companion to Art*.
Oxford University Press, Oxford, 1978.
Perkin, Harold, *The Origins of Modern English
Society 1780–1880*. Routledge & Kegan Paul,
London, 1969.
Pliatzky, Leo, *Getting and Spending*. Blackwell,
Oxford, 1982.
Prebble, John: *The Lion in the North*. Secker &
Warburg, London, 1971.
The Highland Clearances. Secker & Warburg,
London, 1963.
Priestley, J. B., *English Journey*. Heinemann,
London, 1933.
Randle, John, *Understanding Britain*. Blackwell,
Oxford, 1981.
Reader, W. J., *The Middle Class*. Batsford,
London, 1972.
Reid, Ivan, *Social Class Differences in Britain*. Grant
McIntyre, 1981.
Robbins, Keith, *The Eclipse of a Great Power,
Modern Britain 1870–1975*. Longman, London,
1983.
Sampson, Anthony: *The Changing Anatomy of
Britain*. Hodder & Stoughton, Sevenoaks, Kent,
1982.
The Moneylenders. Hodder & Stoughton,
Sevenoaks, Kent, 1981.
Scholes, Percy A., *The Concise Oxford Dictionary of
Music*. Oxford University Press, Oxford, 1977.
Simper, R., *Britain's Maritime Heritage*. David and
Charles, Newton Abbot, Devon, 1982.
Smith, Anthony, *Beside the Seaside*. George Allen &
Unwin, London, 1972.
Smith, Vincent A., *The Oxford History of India*.
Oxford University Press, Oxford, 1958.
Sutherland, Douglas, *The English Gentleman's Wife*.
Debrett's Peerage, 1979.
Taylor, A. J. P.: *English History 1914–45*.
Clarendon Press, Oxford, 1965.
Europe: Grandeur and Decline. Penguin Books,
London, 1976.
Taylor, Robert, *The Fifth Estate: Britain's Unions in
the Modern World*. Pan Books, London, 1980.
Theroux, Paul, *The Kingdom by the Sea: A Journey
around Great Britain*. Hamish Hamilton,
London, 1983.
Thornton, A. P., *The Imperial Idea and its Enemies*.
Macmillan, London, 1959.
de Tocqueville, Alexis, *Journeys to England and*

Ireland. Trans. by G. Lawrence and K. P. Mayer, Faber & Faber, London, 1958.

Trevelyan, G. M.: *A Shortened History of England.* Penguin Books, London, 1959.

English Social History. Longman, London, 1942.

Westergaard, John, and Resler, Henrietta, *Class in a Capitalist Society: A Study of Contemporary Britain.* Heinemann, London, 1975.

Wiener, M. J., *English Culture and the Decline of the Industrial Spirit.* Cambridge University Press, Cambridge, 1981.

Williams, Raymond, *Culture and Society 1780–1950.* Penguin Books, London, 1982.

Wilson, Harold, *The Governance of Britain.* Weidenfeld and Nicolson, London, 1976.

Woodruff, Philip, *The Men who Ruled India.* Vols 1 & 2. Jonathan Cape, London, 1963.

Wormell, Peter, *Anatomy of Agriculture.* Harrap, London, 1978.

Wright, Christopher, *The Working Class.* Batsford, London, 1972.

PERIODICALS

Bell, D., "A Report on England: the Future that never was." *The Public Interest,* no. 51, Spring 1978.

Beloff, Max, "Dream of Commonwealth." *The Round Table,* 1970.

"Britain's Economy Under Strain." *The Economist,* special report, 1982.

Commission of the European Communities, *Eurobarometer,* no. 18, December 1982.

Euromonitor: *World Book News* 1981/2.
The Euromonitor Books Readership Survey 1983.
U.K. Book Report.

Her Majesty's Stationery Office: *Britain 1984: An Official Handbook.*
CSO Annual Abstract of Statistics 1957.
CSO Monthly Digest of Statistics.
Department of Employment Gazette Dec. 1974, Jan. 1979, Mar. 1983, Jan. 1983, Oct. 1975, Feb. 1979.
Economic Trends 1981/1984 edns.
General Household Survey 1982.
OPCS Census 1981.
OPCS Series MN no. 1 International Migration.
Regional Trends 1981/1984 edns.
Social Trends 1981/1984 edns.

Marquand, David, "Trying to Diagnose the British Disease." *Encounter,* December 1980.

Mitford, Nancy, "The English Aristocracy." *Encounter,* September 5, 1955.

Organization for Economic Co-operation and Development:
OECD Economic Surveys, United Kingdom 1982–1983, Feb, 1983.
OECD Observer no. 115, March 1982. no. 127, March 1984.

The Sports Council: *A Digest of Sports Statistics.* ed. B. Duffield, 1982.
Sport in the Community. The Next Ten Years. 1982.

"The Unpredictable Invasion." *The Economist,* January 22, 1983.

INDEX

Colour separations by City Ensign Group, Hull, England.
Typesetting by Tradespools Ltd., Somerset, England.
Printed and bound by Artes Gráficas Toledo, S.A., Spain.
D. L. TO:370-1987

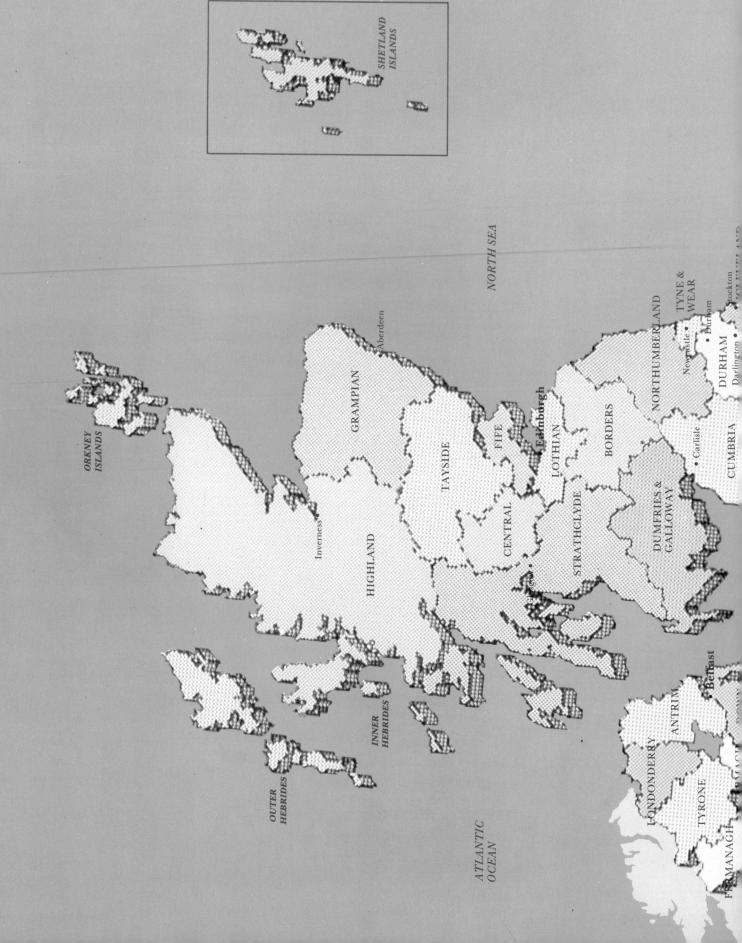